RUSSIAN STATE UNIVERSITY FOR THE HUMANITIES

FACULTY OF HISTORY, POLITICAL SCIENCE AND LAW

RUSSIAN ACADEMY OF SCIENCES

CENTER FOR CIVILIZATIONAL AND REGIONAL STUDIES
INSTITUTE OF ORIENTAL STUDIES

A. Korotayev
A. Malkov
D. Khaltourina

INTRODUCTION
TO SOCIAL
MACRODYNAMICS

Compact Macromodels
of the World System Growth

MOSCOW

URSS

ББК 22.318 60.5

This study has been supported
by the Russian Foundation for the Fundamental Research
(*Projects* № 04–06–8022 and № 02–06–80260)

Korotayev Andrey, Malkov Artemy, Khaltourina Daria

Introduction to Social Macrodynamics: Compact Macromodels of the World System Growth. — M.: KomKniga, 2006. — 128 p.

ISBN 5–484–00414–4

Human society is a complex nonequilibrium system that changes and develops constantly. Complexity, multivariability, and contradictoriness of social evolution lead researchers to a logical conclusion that any simplification, reduction, or neglect of the multiplicity of factors leads inevitably to the multiplication of error and to significant misunderstanding of the processes under study. The view that any simple general laws are not observed at all with respect to social evolution has become totally predominant within the academic community, especially among those who specialize in the Humanities and who confront directly in their research all the manifold unpredictability of social processes. A way to approach human society as an extremely complex system is to recognize differences of abstraction and time scale between different levels. If the main task of scientific analysis is to detect the main forces acting on systems so as to discover fundamental laws at a sufficiently coarse scale, then abstracting from details and deviations from general rules may help to identify measurable deviations from these laws in finer detail and shorter time scales. Modern achievements in the field of mathematical modeling suggest that social evolution can be described with rigorous and sufficiently simple macrolaws.

This book discusses general regularities of the World System growth. It is shown that they can be described mathematically in a rather accurate way with rather simple models.

The text and typesetting of this book have been supplied entirely by the authors.

Издательство «КомКнига». 117312, г. Москва, пр-т 60-летия Октября, 9.
Подписано к печати 12.12.2005 г. Формат 60×90/16. Печ. л. 8. Зак. № 368.
Отпечатано в ООО «ЛЕНАНД». 117312, г. Москва, пр-т 60-летия Октября, д. 11А, стр. 11.

ISBN 5–484–00414–4

SCIENTIFIC LITERATURE AND TEXTBOOKS

E-mail: URSS@URSS.ru
Our catalogue on the Internet:
http://URSS.ru
Phone/fax: 7(095)135–42–16
Phone/fax: 7(095)135–42–46   **URSS**

3756 ID 34250

9 785484 004140 >

Contents

Acknowledgements

First and foremost, our thanks go to the Institute for Advanced Study, Princeton. Without the first author's one-year membership in this Institute this book could hardly have been written. We are also grateful to the Russian Foundation for Basic Research for financial support of this work (projects # 04–06–8022 and # 02-06-80260).

We would like to express our special gratitude to Gregory Malinetsky, Sergey Podlazov (Institute for Applied Mathematics, Russian Academy of Sciences), Robert Graber (Truman State University), Victor de Munck (State University of New York), Duran Bell and Douglas R. White (University of California, Irvine) for their invaluable help and advice.

We would also like to thank our colleagues who offered us useful comments and insights on the subject of this book: Leonid Alaev (Oriental Institute, Russian Academy of Sciences), Herbert Barry III (University of Pittsburgh), Yuri Berzkin (Kunstkammer, St. Petersburg), Svetlana Borinskaya (Institute of General Genetics, Russian Academy of Sciences), Dmitri Bondarenko (Institute for African Studies, Russian Academy of Sciences), Michael L. Burton (University of California, Irvine), Robert L. Carneiro (American Museum of Natural History, New York), Henry J. M. Claessen (Leiden University), Marina Butovskaya (Institute of Ethnology and Anthroplogy, Russian Academy of Sciences), Dmitrij Chernavskij (Institute of Physics, Russian Academy of Sciences), Marat Cheshkov (Institute of International Economics, Russian Academy of Sciences), Loren Demerath (Centenary College), Georgi and Lubov Derlouguian (Northwestern University, Evanston), William T. Divale (City University of New York), Timothy K. Earle (Northwestern University), Leonid Grinin (Center for Social and Historical Research, Volgograd), Eric C. Jones (University of North Carolina), Natalia Komarova (University of California, Irvine), Sergey Nefedov (Russian Academy of Sciences, Ural Branch, Ekaterinburg), Nikolay Kradin (Russian Academy of Sciences, Far East Branch, Vladivostok), Vitalij Meliantsev (Institute of Asia and Africa, Moscow State University), Akop Nazaretyan (Oriental Institute, Russian Academy of Sciences), Nikolay Rozov (Novosibirsk State University), Igor Sledzevski (Institute for African Studies, Moscow), David Small (Lehigh University), Peter Turchin (University of Connecticut, Storrs), and Paul Wason (Templeton Foundation).

Needless to say, faults, mistakes, infelicities, *etc.*, are our own responsibility.

Introduction[1]

Human society is a complex nonequilibrium system that changes and develops constantly. Complexity, multivariability, and contradictoriness of social evolution lead researchers to a logical conclusion that any simplification, reduction, or neglect of the multiplicity of factors leads inevitably to the multiplication of error and to significant misunderstanding of the processes under study. The view that any simple general laws are not observed at all with respect to social evolution has become totally predominant within the academic community, especially among those who specialize in the Humanities and who confront directly in their research all the manifold unpredictability of social processes.

A way to approach human society as an extremely complex system is to recognize differences of abstraction and time scale between different levels. If the main task of scientific analysis is to detect the main forces acting on systems so as to discover fundamental laws at a sufficiently coarse scale, then abstracting from details and deviations from general rules may help to identify measurable deviations from these laws in finer detail and shorter time scales. Modern achievements in the field of mathematical modeling suggest that social evolution can be described with rigorous and sufficiently simple macrolaws. Our goal, at this stage, is to discuss a family of mathematical models whose greater specification leads to measurable variables and testable relationships.

Tremendous successes and spectacular developments in physics (especially, in comparison with other sciences) were, to a considerable degree, connected with the fact that physics managed to achieve a synthesis of mathematical methods and subject knowledge. Notwithstanding the fact that already in the classical world physical theories achieved a rather high level, it was in the modern era that the introduction of mathematics made it possible to penetrate deeper into the essence of physical laws, laying the ground for the scientific-technological revolution. However, such a synthesis was not possible without one important condition. Mathematics operates with forms and numbers, and, hence, the physical world had to be translated into the language of forms and numbers. It demanded the development of effective methods for measuring physical values and the introduction of scales and measures. Starting with the simplest variables – length, mass, time – physicists learned how to measure

---

[1] This book is a translation of an amended and enlarged version of Part 1 of the following monograph originally published in Russian: Коротаев, А. В., А. С. Малков и Д. А. Халтурина. *Законы истории: Математическое моделирование исторических макропроцессов (Демография. Экономика. Войны)*. М.: УРСС, 2005.

charge, viscosity, inductance, spin and many other variables, which are necessary for the development of the physical theory of value.

In an analogous way, a constructive synthesis of the social sciences with mathematics calls for the introduction of adequate methods for the measurement of social variables. In the social sciences, as in physics, some variables can be measured relatively easily, while the measurement of some other variables needs additional research and even the development of auxiliary models.

One social variable that is relatively well accessible to direct measurement is population size. That is why it is not surprising that the field of demography attracts the special attention of social scientists, as it suggests some hope for the development of quantitatively based scientific theories. It is remarkable that the penetration of mathematical methods into biology began, to a considerable extent, with the description of population dynamics.

The basic measurability of data is quite evident here; what is more, the basic equation for the description of demographic dynamics is also rather evident, as it stems from the conservation law:

$$\frac{dN}{dt} = B - D,$$

(0.1)

where N is the number of people, B is the number of births, and D is the number of deaths in the unit of time. However, at the microlevel it turns out that both the number of deaths and number of births depend heavily on a huge number of social parameters, including the "human factor" – decisions made by individual people that are very difficult to formalize.

In addition to this, equation (0.1) does not take into account the spatial movement of people; hence, it should be extended:

$$\frac{\partial N}{\partial t} = B - D - \text{div}\mathbf{J},$$

(0.1')

where vector $\mathbf{J}$ corresponds to the migration current. In this case the problem becomes even more complicated, as migration processes are even more likely to be influenced by external factors.

That is why any formal description of demographic processes at the microlevel confronts serious problems associated first of all with the lack of sufficient research on formal social laws connecting economic, political, ethical and other factors that affect individual and small group (*e.g.*, household or nuclear family) behavior. Thus, at the moment the only available approach is macrolevel description that does not go into the fine details of demographic processes and describes dynamics of very large human populations, which is influenced by the human factor at a significantly coarser level of abstraction and on a longer time-scale.

Biological processes of birth and death are characteristic not only of people, but also of any animals. That is why a rather natural step is to try to describe demographic models using population models developed within biology (see, e.g., Riznichenko 2002).

The basic model describing animal population dynamics is the logistic model, suggested by Verhulst (1838):

$$\frac{dN}{dt} = rN(1 - \frac{N}{K}), \qquad (0.2)$$

which can be also presented in the following way:

$$\frac{dN}{dt} = (a_1 N) - (a_2 N + bN^2), \qquad (0.3)$$

where $a_1 N$ corresponds to the number of births B, and $a_2 N + bN^2$ corresponds to the number of deaths in equation (0.1); r, K, a_1, a_2, b are positive coefficients connected between themselves by the following relationships:

$$r = a_1 - a_2 \quad \text{and} \quad b = \frac{r}{K}, \qquad (0.4)$$

The logic of equation (0.3) is as follows: fertility a_1 is a constant; thus, the number of births $B = a_1 N$ is proportional to the population size, natural death rate a_2 is also considered to be constant, whereas quadratic addition bN^2 in expression for full number of deaths $D = a_1 N + bN^2$ appears due to the resource limitation, which does not let population grow infinitely. Coefficient b is called the coefficient of interspecies competition.

As a result, the population dynamics described by the logistic equation has the following characteristics. At the beginning, when the size of the animal population size is low, we observe an exponential growth with exponent $r = a_1 - a_2$. Then, as the ecological niche is being filled, the population growth slows down, and finally the population comes to the constant level K.

The value of parameter K, called the *carrying capacity of an ecological niche for the given population*, is of principal importance. This value determines the equilibrium state in population dynamics for the given resource limitations and controls the limits of its growth.

Another well known population dynamics model is Lotka – Volterra one (Lotka 1925; Volterra 1926), denoted also as the "prey – predator" model. It describes dynamics of populations of two interacting species, one of which constitutes the main food resource for the other, and consists of two equations of type (0.1):

$$\frac{dx}{dt} = Ax - Bxy$$

$$\frac{dy}{dt} = Cxy - Dy,$$

(0.5)

where x is the size of the prey population, y is the size of the predator population; A, B, C, D are coefficients.

This model, like (0.2), assumes that the number of prey births is proportional to their population size. The number of predator deaths is also proportional to their population size. As regards prey death rates and predator fertility rates, we are dealing here with a system effect. Prey animals are assumed to die mainly because of contacts with predators, whereas the predator fertility rates depend on the availability of food – prey animals. The model assumes that the average number of contacts between prey animals and predators depends mainly on the size of both populations and suggests expression Bxy for the number of prey deaths and Cxy for the number of predator births.

This model generates a cyclical dynamics. The growth of the prey population leads to the growth of the predator population; the growth of predator population leads to the decrease of the prey animal number; decrease of the prey population leads to the decrease of the predators' number; and when the number of predators is very small, the prey population can grow very rapidly.

The population models described above are used very widely in biological research. It seems reasonable to suppose that, as humans have a biological nature, some relations similar to the ones described above, or their analogues could be valid for humans too.

In deep prehistory, when human ancestors did not differ much from animals, models (0.2) – (0.4) may have been applied to them without any significant reservations. However, with the appearance of a new human environment, the sociotechnological one, the direct application of those models does not appear to be entirely adequate. In particular, model (0.2) assumes carrying capacity to be determined by exogenous factors; however, human history shows that over the course of time the carrying capacity of land has tended to increase in a rather significant way. Hence, in long-range perspective carrying capacity cannot be assumed to be constant and determined entirely by exogenous conditions. Humans are capable of transforming those conditions affecting carrying capacity.

As regards model (0.4), it has an extremely limited applicability to humans in its direct form, as humans learned how to defend themselves effectively from predators at very early stages of their evolution; hence, humans cannot function as "prey" in this model. On the other hand, humans learned how not to depend on the fluctuations of prey animals populations, hence, they cannot function as predators because in model (0.4) predators are very sensitive to the variations of prey animal numbers (This model could still have some limited direct applicability to a very few cases of highly specialized hunters).

However, model (0.4) may find a new non-traditional application in demographic models. In particular it may be applied to the description of demographic cycles that have been found in historical dynamics of almost all the agrarian societies, for which relevant data are available. The population plays here the role of "prey", whereas the role of "predator" belongs to sociopolitical instability, internal warfare, famines and epidemics whose probability increases when an increasing population approaches the carrying capacity ceiling (for detail see, *e.g.*, Korotayev, Malkov and Khaltourina 2005: 211–54). Demographic cycles are by themselves a very interesting subject for mathematical research, and they have been studied rather actively in recent years (Usher 1989; Chu and Lee 1994; Malkov and Sergeev 2002, 2004; Malkov *et al.* 2002; Malkov 2002, 2003, 2004; Malkov, Selunskaja, and Sergeev 2005; Turchin 2003; Turchin and Korotayev 2006; Nefedov 2002a; 2004; Korotayev, Malkov and Khaltourina 2005 *etc.*)

As is well known in complexity studies, chaotic dynamics at the microlevel can generate a highly deterministic macrolevel behavior (*e.g.*, Chernavskij 2004). To describe behavior of a few dozen gas molecules in a closed vessel we need very complex mathematical models; and these models would still be unable to predict long-run dynamics of such a system due to inevitable irreducible chaotic components. However, the behavior of zillions of gas molecules can be described with extremely simple sets of equations, which are capable of predicting almost perfectly the macrodynamics of all the basic parameters (just because of chaotic behavior at microlevel). Of course, one cannot fail to wonder whether a similar set of regularities would not also be observed in the human world too. That is, cannot a few very simple equations account for an extremely high proportion of all the macrovariation with respect to the largest possible social system – the World System?

Chapter 1

Macrotrends of World Population Growth

The world population growth in 1950–2003 had the following shape (see Diagram 1.1[1]):

Diagram 1.1. World Population Growth, 1950–2003 (millions)

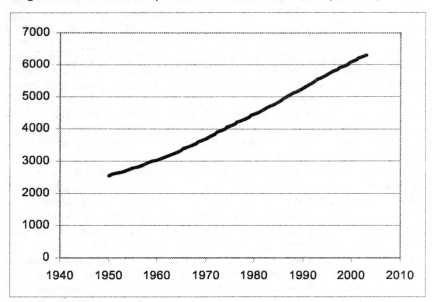

Though at first glance world population growth in 1950–2003 looks almost perfectly linear, even a very simple analysis of the dynamics of annual growth rates indicates that the actual situation is far more complex (see Table 1.1 and Diagram 1.2):

---

[1] The world population dynamics data for 1950–2003 are here and elsewhere from US Census Bureau database (2004).

Table 1. World Population Dynamics, 1950–2003

Year	Population	Annual growth rate (%)	Annual population change
1950	2,555,360,972	1.47	37,785,986
1951	2,593,146,958	1.61	42,060,389
1952	2,635,207,347	1.71	45,337,232
1953	2,680,544,579	1.77	47,971,823
1954	2,728,516,402	1.87	51,451,629
1955	2,779,968,031	1.89	52,959,308
1956	2,832,927,339	1.95	55,827,050
1957	2,888,754,389	1.94	56,506,563
1958	2,945,260,952	1.76	52,335,100
1959	2,997,596,052	1.39	42,073,278
1960	3,039,669,330	1.33	40,792,172
1961	3,080,461,502	1.80	56,094,590
1962	3,136,556,092	2.19	69,516,194
1963	3,206,072,286	2.19	71,119,813
1964	3,277,192,099	2.08	69,031,982
1965	3,346,224,081	2.08	70,238,858
1966	3,416,462,939	2.02	69,755,364
1967	3,486,218,303	2.04	71,882,406
1968	3,558,100,709	2.08	74,679,905
1969	3,632,780,614	2.05	75,286,491
1970	3,708,067,105	2.07	77,587,001
1971	3,785,654,106	2.01	76,694,660
1972	3,862,348,766	1.95	76,183,283
1973	3,938,532,049	1.90	75,547,218
1974	4,014,079,267	1.81	73,271,828
1975	4,087,351,095	1.74	71,804,569
1976	4,159,155,664	1.72	72,229,696
1977	4,231,385,360	1.69	72,172,075
1978	4,303,557,435	1.73	75,085,858
1979	4,378,643,293	1.72	75,746,226

Year	Population	Annual growth rate (%)	Annual population change
1980	4,454,389,519	1.68	75,430,353
1981	4,529,819,872	1.74	79,706,283
1982	4,609,526,155	1.75	81,444,423
1983	4,690,970,578	1.70	80,459,709
1984	4,771,430,287	1.70	81,822,376
1985	4,853,252,663	1.71	83,561,368
1986	4,936,814,031	1.73	86,175,601
1987	5,022,989,632	1.71	86,843,511
1988	5,109,833,143	1.69	86,965,235
1989	5,196,798,378	1.68	87,880,745
1990	5,284,679,123	1.58	84,130,498
1991	5,368,809,621	1.56	84,182,087
1992	5,452,991,708	1.49	81,942,247
1993	5,534,933,955	1.44	80,547,532
1994	5,615,481,487	1.43	80,781,974
1995	5,696,263,461	1.38	79,253,622
1996	5,775,517,083	1.37	79,551,074
1997	5,855,068,157	1.32	78,019,039
1998	5,933,087,196	1.29	76,861,716
1999	6,009,948,912	1.25	75,529,866
2000	6,085,478,778	1.21	74,220,528
2001	6,159,699,306	1.18	73,002,863
2002	6,232,702,169	1.16	72,442,511
2003	6,305,144,680	1.14	72,496,962

Diagram 1.2. Dynamics of Annual World Population Growth, 1950–2003 (%)

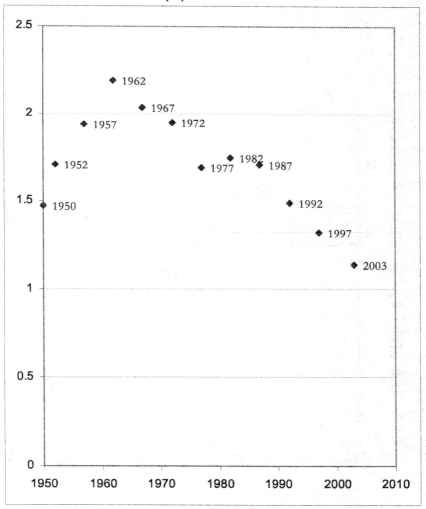

As we see, before 1962 one can observe a rather rapid increase of population growth rates. However after 1963 we encounter a clear-cut reverse trend – the annual growth rates tend to decrease rather steadily and fast. In fact in 1990–2003 we observe an extremely strong negative correlation between world population and world population growth rates (see Diagram 1.3):

Diagram 1.3.   Correlation between World Population Size and
World Population Annual Growth Rate, 1990–2003

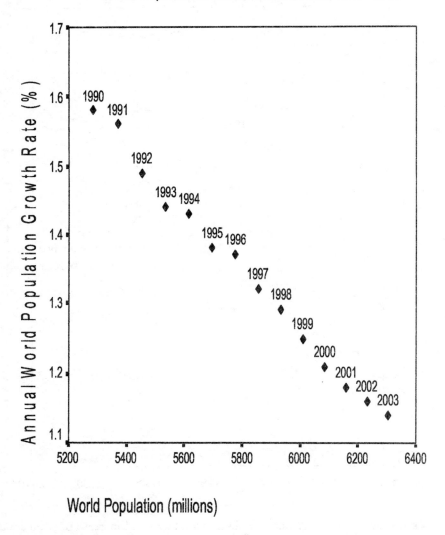

World Population (millions)

Regression analysis of this dataset gives the following results (see Table 1.2):

Table 1.2. Correlation between World Population Size and
World Population Annual Growth Rate, 1990–2003
(regression analysis)

Model	Unstandardized Coefficients		Standardized Coefficients	t	Sig.
	B	Std. Error	Beta		
(Constant)	3.903	0.064		61.290	0.0000000000000003
1 World Population (billions)	-0.441	0.011	-0.996	-40.259	0.00000000000004
Dependent Variable: **World Population Annual Growth Rate (%)**					

NOTE: $R = 0.996$, $R^2 = 0.993$.

This, of course, suggests that 99.3% of all the world macrodemographic variation in 1990–2003 is predicted by the following extremely simple equation:

$$r = 3.9 - 0.44N, \tag{1.1}$$

where N is the world population in billions, and r is the annual population growth rate (%).

Naturally, this makes it possible to estimate what the future population of the world will be if the recent pattern of relationships between N and r persists, using the following equation (Model 1):

Model 1

$$N_{i+1} = N_i (1 + [3.9 - 0.44N_i]/100)$$

The results of respective simulation starting in 2003 with $N = 6,305,144,680$ look as follows (see Table 1.3 and Diagram 1.4):

Table 1.3. Future Population (millions) of the World,
estimates produced with Model 1 simulation

Year	2010	2020	2030	2040	2050	2060	2070
Population	6785.6	7360.3	7801.6	8126.0	8356.8	8517.2	8626.8
Year	2080	2090	2100	2110	2120	2130	2150
Population	8700.9	8750.6	8783.8	8805.8	8820.5	8830.2	8840.8

Diagram 4. World Population (millions) in 1950–2003,
with Extrapolation of 1990–2003 Dynamic Trend till 2150

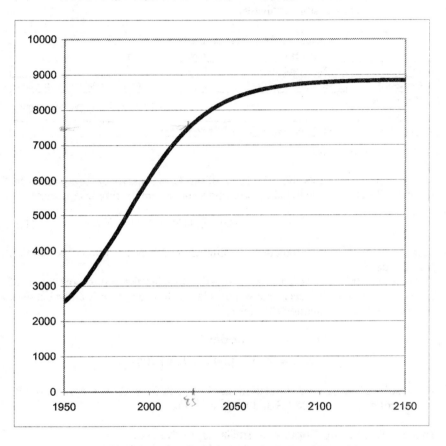

How likely is it that actual world population growth will follow this pattern? As we shall see, there are strong theoretical and empirical grounds to maintain that in no way is this entirely unlikely.

To start with, the pattern of strong linear relationship between world population size and world population growth rate observed for 1990–2003 is in no way unique for the world's demographic history. In fact, just this pattern prevailed for most of human history, at least within the last two millennia (*e.g.*, Kapitza 1992, 1999; Kremer 1993). For example, for 1650–1960 this relationship looks as follows (see Table 1.4 and Diagram 1.5):

Table 1.4. World Population Macrodynamics, 1650–2003

Period	World Population at the beginning of the Period (millions)	Average Annual Growth Rate during the Respective Period (%)
1650-1700	545.0	0.2253
1700-1750	610.0	0.3316
1750-1800	720.0	0.4463
1800-1850	900.0	0.5754
1850-1875	1200.0	0.3964
1875-1900	1325.0	0.8164
1900-1920	1625.0	0.8306
1920-1930	1813.0	0.9164
1930-1940	1987.0	1.0777
1940-1950	2213.0	1.2832
1950-1960	2555.4	1.8226
1960-1970	3039.7	2.0151

NOTE: estimates by (Kremer 1993: 683).

Diagram 1.5. Correlation between World Population Size and World Population Annual Growth Rate, 1650–1970

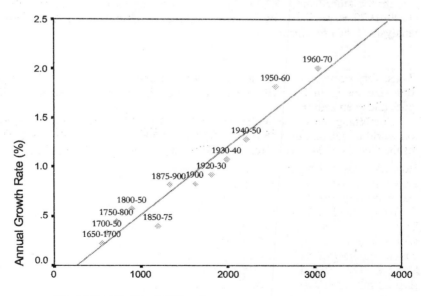

Regression analysis of Kremer's dataset for 1650–1970 produces the following results (see Table 1.5):

Table 1.5. Correlation between World Population Size and World Population Annual Growth Rate, 1650–1970 (regression analysis)

Model	Unstandardized Coefficients		Standardized Coefficients	t	Sig.
	B	Std. Error	Beta		
2 (Constant)	-0.172	0.099		-1.744	0.112
World Population (billions)	0.691	0.057	0.967	12.074	0.0000003
Dependent Variable: **World Population Annual Growth Rate** (%)					

NOTE: $R = 0.967$, $R^2 = 0.936$ (for 1900-1970 $R = 0.981$, $R^2 = 0.962$)

This, of course, suggests that 93.6% of all the world macrodemographic variation in 1650–1970 is predicted by another simple equation (Model 2):

$$r = 0.69N - 0.17,$$

where N is the world population in billions, and r is the annual population growth rate.

On the other hand, 96.2 % of all the world macrodemographic variation in 1900–1970 is predicted by Model 3 arrived at through a similar regression analysis of data for this period:

$$r = 0.92N - 0.71 .$$

Thus, very strong and rather uniform linear relationship between world population size and annual growth rate can be observed in historical record for decades and even centuries.

Combining our extrapolation of 1990-2003 world population with the data on world population growth from 500 BCE till 2003 (Kremer 1993; US Bureau of the Census 2004)[2] we arrive at the following picture (see Diagram 1.6):

---

[2] The other sources consulted are: Thomlinson 1975; Durand 1977; McEvedy and Jones 1978: 342–51; Biraben 1980; Haub 1995: 5; UN Population Division 2004; World Bank 2004.

Diagram 1.6.   World Population Growth, 500 BCE – 2300 CE, millions

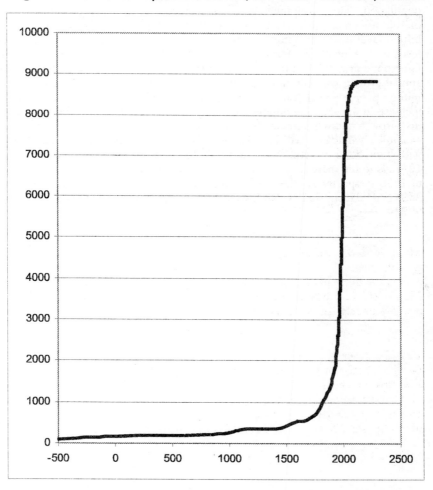

In fact there is only one really significant difference in the patterns of world population growth observed in 1990–2003, on the one hand, and in the pre-1962/3 era, on the other. In 1990–2003 we observe a very strong NEGATIVE correlation between world population size and annual growth rates. For the pre-1962/3 era we also find a very strong correlation between those two variables. But this correlation is POSITIVE.

Naturally, this means that the long-run world population growth trend in the pre-1962/3 era was HYPERBOLIC. The hyperbolic population growth implies that the absolute population growth is proportional to the square of population (unlike exponential growth when the absolute growth is lineally proportional to population). Thus, with the exponential growth if at the world population level of 100 million the absolute annual growth was 100 thousand people a year, at 1 billion level it will be 1 million people a year (a ten times growth of population leads to an equivalent 10 times increase in the absolute population growth). For hyperbolic growth, if at the world population level of 100 million the absolute annual growth was 100 thousand people a year, at 1 billion level it will be 10 million people a year (the ten times growth of population leads to a 100 times increase in the absolute population growth rate). Note that the relative population growth rate will remain constant with the exponential growth (0.1% in our example), whereas it will be lineally proportional to absolute population level with hyperbolic growth (in our example the population growth by a factor of 10 leads to the increase in the relative annual growth rate 10 times, from 0.1% to 1%). Respectively, the world population growth trend observed in 1990–2003 can be identified as INVERSE HYPERBOLIC (or just logistic).

Chapter 2

A Compact Macromodel of World Population Growth

The fact that up to the 1960s world population growth had been characterized by a hyperbolic trend was discovered quite long ago (see, *e.g.*, von Foerster, Mora, and Amiot 1960; von Hoerner 1975; Kremer 1993; Kapitza 1992, 1999, *etc.*). In 1960 von Foerster, Mora, and Amiot conducted a statistical analysis of the available world population data and found out that the general shape of the world population (N) growth is best approximated by the curve described by the following equation:

$$ N = \frac{C}{t_0 - t}, \tag{2.1} $$

where C and t_0 are constants, whereas t_0 corresponds to an absolute limit of such a trend at which N would become infinite, and thus logically implies the certainty of the empirical conclusion that further increases in the growth trend will cease well before that date, which von Foerster wryly called the "doomsday" implication of power-law growth (he refers tongue-in-cheek to the estimated t_0 as "Doomsday, Friday, 13 November, A.D. 2026").

Von Foerster, Mora, and Amiot try to account for their empirical observations by modifying the usual starting equations (0.1) and (0.3) for population dynamics, so as to describe the process under consideration:

$$ \frac{dN}{dt} = B - D, \tag{0.1} $$

where N is the number of people, B is the number of births, and D is the number of deaths in the unit of time;

$$\frac{dN}{dt} = (a_1 N) - (a_2 N + bN^2), \tag{0.3}$$

where $a_1 N$ corresponds to the number of births B, and $a_2 N + bN^2$ corresponds to the number of deaths in equation (0.1); let us recollect that r, K, a_1, a_2, b are positive coefficients connected between themselves by the following relationships:

$$r = a_1 - a_2 \quad \text{and} \quad b = \frac{r}{K}, \tag{0.4}$$

They start with the observation that when individuals in a population compete in a limited environment, the growth rate typically *decreases* with the greater number N in competition. This situation would typically apply where sufficient communication is lacking to enable resort to other than a competitive and nearly zero-sum multiperson game. It might not apply, they suppose, when the elements in a population "possess a system of communication which enables them to form coalitions" and especially when "all elements are so strongly linked that the population as a whole can be considered from a game-theoretical point of view as a single person playing a two-person game with nature as the opponent" (von Foerster, Mora, and Amiot 1960: 1292). Thus, the larger the population (N^k coalition members, where $k \le 1$) the more the decrease of natural risks and the higher the population growth rate. They suggest modeling such a situation through the introduction of nonlinearity in the following form:

$$\frac{dN}{dt} = (a_0 N^{\frac{1}{k}}) N, \tag{2.2}$$

where a_0 and k are constants, which should be determined experimentally. The analysis of experimental data by von Foerster, Mora, and Amiot determines values $a_0 = 5.5 \times 10^{-12}$ and $k = 0.99$ that produce the hyperbolic equation for world population growth:

$$N = N_1 \left(\frac{t_0 - t_1}{t_0 - t} \right)^k, \tag{2.3}$$

which, assuming $k = 1.0$ (von Hoerner1975) is written more succinctly as (2.1) and in equivalent form (Kapitza 1992, 1999) as (2.4):[1]

$$\frac{dN}{dt} = \frac{N^2}{C}.$$

(2.4)

Though von Foerster's, von Hoerner's and Kapitza's models produce a phenomenal fit with the empirical data, they do not account for mechanisms of the hyperbolic trend; as we shall see in the next chapter, Kremer's (1993) model accounts for it, but it is rather complex. In fact, the general shape of world population growth dynamics could be accounted for with strikingly simple models like the one we would like to propose ourselves below (or the model proposed by Tsirel [2004]).[2]

With Kremer (1993), Komlos, Nefedov (2002) and others (Habakkuk 1953; Postan 1950, 1972; Braudel 1973; Abel 1974, 1980; Cameron 1989; Artzrouni and Komlos 1985 *etc.*), we make "the Malthusian (1978) assumption that population is limited by the available technology, so that the growth rate of population is proportional to the growth rate of technology" (Kremer 1993: 681–2),[3] and that, on the other hand, "high population spurs technological change because it increases the number of potential inventors...[4] In a larger population there will be proportionally more people lucky or smart enough to come up with new ideas"[5] (Kremer 1993: 685), thus, "the growth rate of technology is proportional to total population"[6] (Kremer 1993: 682; see also, *e.g.*, Kuznets 1960; Grossman and Helpman 1991; Aghion and Howitt 1992, 1998; Simon 1977, 1981, 2000; Komlos and Nefedov 2002; Jones 1995, 2003, 2005 *etc.*).

---

[1] See Appendix 3 for more detail.

[2] For other models of the world population hyperbolic growth see Cohen 1995; Johansen and Sornette 2001; Podlazov 2004.

[3] In addition to this, the absolute growth rate is proportional to population itself – with the given relative growth rate a larger population will increase more in absolute numbers than a smaller one.

[4] "This implication flows naturally from the nonrivalry of technology... The cost of inventing a new technology is independent of the number of people who use it. Thus, holding constant the share of resources devoted to research, an increase in population leads to an increase in technological change" (Kremer 1993: 681).

[5] The second assumption is in fact Boserupian rather than Malthusian (Boserup 1965; Lee 1986).

[6] Note that "the growth rate of technology" means here the relative growth rate (*i.e.*, the level to which technology will grow in the given unit of time in proportion to the level observed at the beginning of this period). This, of course, implies that the absolute speed of technology growth in the given period of time will be proportional not only to the population size, but also to the absolute technology level at the beginning of this period.

The simplest way to model mathematically the relationships between these two subsystems (which, up to our knowledge, has not yet been proposed)[7] is to use the following set of differential equations:

$$\frac{dN}{dt} = a(bK - N)N, \tag{2.5}$$

$$\frac{dK}{dt} = cNK, \tag{2.6}$$

where N is the world population, K is the level of technology; bK corresponds to the number of people (N), which the earth can support with the given level of technology (K). With such a compact model we are able to reproduce rather well the long-run hyperbolic growth of world population before 1962-3.

With our two-equation model we start the simulation in the year 1650 and do annual iterations with difference equations derived from the differential ones:

$K_{i+1} = K_i + cN_iK_i$,
$N_{i+1} = N_i + a(bK_{i+1} - N_i)N_i$.

We choose the following values for the constants and initial conditions: $N = 0.0545$ of tens of billions (*i.e.* 545 million)[8]; $a = 1;$ $b = 1;$ $K = 0.0545;$[9] $c = 0.05135$. The outcome of the simulation, presented in Diagrams 2.1–2 indicates that irrespective of its simplicity the model is actually capable of replicating quite reasonably the population estimates of Kremer (1993), US Bureau of the Census (2004) and other sources (Thomlinson 1975; Durand 1977; McEvedy and Jones 1978: 342–51; Biraben 1980; Haub 1995: 5; UN Population Division 2005; World Bank 2005) in most of their characteristics and in terms of the important turning points:

[7] The closest proposed model is the one by Tsirel (2004); see our discussion of this very interesting model in Korotayev, Malkov, and Khaltourina 2005: 38–57.
[8] We chose to calculate the world population in tens of billions (rather than, say, in millions) to minimize the rounding error stemming from discrete computer nature (which was to be taken most seriously into account in our case, as the object of modeling had evident characteristics of a blow-up regime).
[9] To simplify the calculations we chose value "1" for both a and b; thus, K in our simulations was measured directly as the number of people which can be supported by the Earth with the given level of technology.

Diagram 2.1.   Predicted and Observed Dynamics
of the World Population Growth,
in millions (1650–1962 CE)

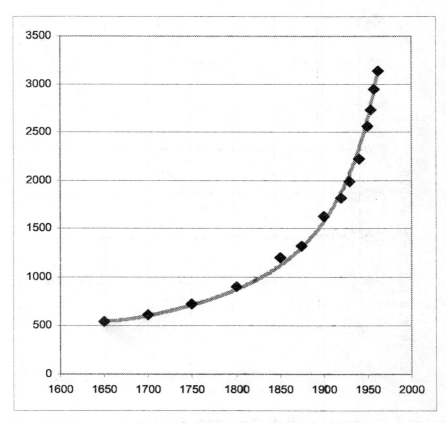

NOTE: The solid grey curve has been generated by the model; black markers correspond to the estimates of world population by Kremer (1993) for pre-1950 period, and US Bureau of Census (2005) world population data for 1950–1962.

The correlation between the predicted and observed values for this simulation looks as follows: $R = 0.9989$, $R^2 = 0.9978$, $p \ll 0.0001$, which, of course, indicate an unusually high fit for such a simple model designed to account for demographic macrodynamics of the most complex social system (see Diagram 2.2):

Diagram 2.2.   Correlation between Predicted and Observed Values
(1650–1962)

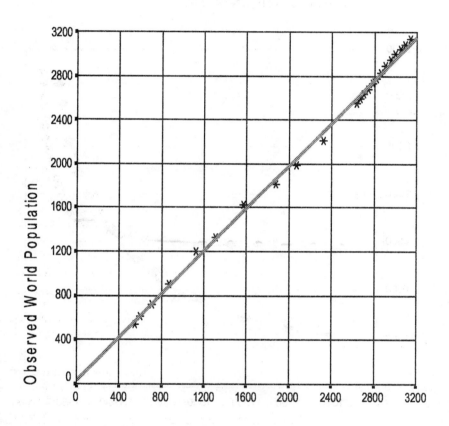

World Population Predicted by the Model

We start our second simulation in the year 500 BCE. In this case we choose the
following values of the constants and initial conditions: $N = 0.01$ of tens of billions (*i.e.* 100 million); $a = 1$; $b = 1$; $K = 0.01$; $c = 0.04093$. The outcome of the
simulation, presented in Diagrams 2.3–4 indicates that irrespective of its extreme simplicity the model is still quite capable of replicating rather reasonably
the population estimates of Kremer (1993), US Bureau of the Census (2004)
and other sources in most of their characteristics and in terms of the important
turning points even for such a long period of time:

Diagram 2.3.   Predicted and Observed Dynamics of the World Population Growth, in millions (500 BCE – 1962 CE)

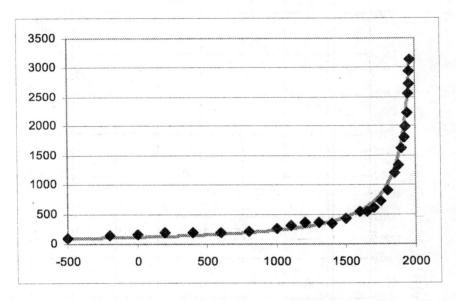

NOTE: The solid grey curve has been generated by the model; black markers correspond to the estimates of world population by Kremer (1993) for pre-1950 period, and US Bureau of Census (2005) world population data for 1950–1962.

The correlation between the predicted and observed values for this simulation looks as follows: $R = 0.9983$, $R^2 = 0.9966$, $p \ll 0.0001$, which, of course, again indicate an unusually high fit for such a simple model designed to account for demographic macrodynamics of the most complex social system for *c.* 2500 years (see Diagram 2.4):

Diagram 2.4.   Correlation between Predicted and Observed Values

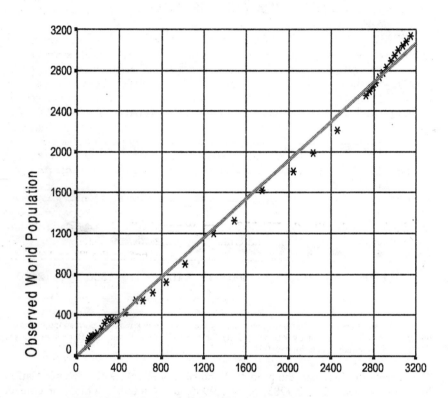

World Population Predicted by the Model

Note that even when the simulation was started *c.* 25000 BCE, it still produced a fit with observed data as high as 0.981 ($R^2 = 0.962$, $p \ll 0.0001$).[10]

Thus, it turns out that the set of two differential equations specified above accounts for 96.2 per cent of all the variation in demographic macrodynamics of the world in the last 25 millennia; it also accounts for 99.66% of this macrovariation in 500 BCE – 1962 CE, and it does for 99.78% in 1650–1962 CE.

---

[10] The simulation was started in the 24939 BCE and done with 269 centennial iterations ending in 1962 CE. In this case we chose the following values of the constants and initial conditions: $N = 0.00334$ billion (*i.e.* 3.34 million); $a = 1$; $b = 1$; $K = 0.00334$; $c = 2.13$.

In fact, we believe this may not be a coincidence that the compact macro-model shows such a high correlation between the predicted and observed data just for 500 BCE – 1962 CE. But why does the correlation significantly decline if the pre-500 BCE period is taken into account?

To start with, when we first encountered models of world population growth, we felt a strong suspicion about them. Indeed, such models imply that the world population can be treated as a system. However, at a certain level of analysis one may doubt if this makes any sense at all. The fact is that up until recently (especially before 1492) humankind did not constitute any real system, as, for example. The growth of the Old World, New World, Australia, Tasmania, or Hawaii populations took place almost perfectly independently of each other. For example, it seems entirely clear that demographic processes in, say, West Eurasia in the 1st millennium CE did not have the slightest impact on the demographic dynamics of the Tasmanian population during the same time period.

However, we believe that the patterns observed in pre-Modern world population growth are not coincidental at all. In fact, they reflect population dynamics of quite a real entity, the World System. We are inclined to speak, with Andre Gunder Frank (*e.g.*, Frank and Gills 1994) but not with Wallerstein (1974), about a single World System which originated long before the "long 16th century".

Note that the presence of a more or less well integrated World System, comprising most of the world population, is a necessary pre-condition for the high correlation between the world population numbers generated by our model and the observed ones. For example, suppose we encounter a case when the world population of N grew 4-fold but got split into 4 perfectly isolated regional populations comprising N persons each. Of course, our model predicts that a 4-fold increase of the world population would tend to lead to a 4-fold increase in the relative world technological growth rate. But have we any grounds to expect to find this in the case specified above? Of course not. Yes, even in this case a four times higher number of people are likely to produce 4 times more innovations. However, the effect predicted by our model would be only observed if innovations produced by any of the four regional populations were shared among all the other populations. However, if we assumed that the four respective populations lived in perfect isolation from each other, then such sharing would not take place, and the expected increase in technological growth rate would not be observed, thereby producing a huge gap between the predictions generated by our model and actually observed data.

It seems that this was just the 1st millennium BCE when the World System integration reached a qualitatively new level. A strong symptom of this seems to be the "Iron Revolution", as a result of which the iron metallurgy spread within a few centuries (not millennia!) throughout a huge space stretching from the Atlantic to the Pacific, producing (as was already supposed by Jaspers

[1953]) a number of important unidirectional transformations in all the main centers of the emerging World System (the Circummediterranean region, Middle East, South Asia, and East Asia), after which the development of each of those centers cannot be adequately understood, described and modeled without taking into consideration the fact that it was a part of a larger and perfectly real whole – the World System.

A few other points seem to be relevant here. Of course, there would be no grounds to speak about the World System stretching from the Atlantic to the Pacific even at the beginning of the 1st Millennium CE if we applied the "bulk-good" criterion suggested by Wallerstein (1974), as there was no movement of bulk goods at all between, say, China and Europe at this time (as we have no grounds not to agree with Wallerstein in his classification of the 1st century Chinese silk reaching Europe as a luxury, rather than a bulk good). However, the 1st century CE (and even the 1st millennium BCE) World System would definitely qualify as such if we apply a "softer" information network criterion suggested by Chase-Dunn and Hall (1997). Note that at our level of analysis, the presence of an information network covering the whole World System is a perfectly sufficient condition, which makes it possible to consider this system as a single evolving entity. Yes, in the 1st millennium BCE any bulk goods could hardly penetrate from the Pacific coast of Eurasia to its Atlantic coast. However, by that time the World System had reached such a level of integration that, say, iron metallurgy could spread through the whole World System within a few centuries.

The other point is that even in the 1st century CE the World System still covered far less than 50% of all the Earth's terrain. However, what seems to be far more important is that already by the beginning of the 1st century CE more than 90% of all the world population lived in just those regions which were constituent parts of the 1st century CE World System (the Circummediterranean region, Middle East, South, Central and East Asia) (see, e.g., Durand 1977: 256). Hence, since the 1st millennium BCE the dynamics of world population reflects very closely just the dynamics of the World System population.

On the other hand, it might not be coincidental that the hyperbolic growth trend may still be traced back to 25000 BCE. Of course, we do not insist on the existence of anything like the World System, say, around 15000 BP. Note, however, that there does not seem to be any evidence for hyperbolic world population growth in 40000 – 10000 BCE. In fact the hyperbolic effect within the 25 millennia BCE is produced by world population dynamics in the last 10 millennia of this period that fits the mathematical model specified above rather well (though not as well, as the world population dynamics in 500 BCE – 1962 CE [let alone 1650 – 1962 CE]).

The simulation for 10000 – 500 BCE was done with the following constants and initial conditions: N = 0.0004 of tens of billions (i.e. 4 million); a = 1; b = 1; K = 0.0004; c = 0.32.

The outcome of the simulation, presented in Diagram 2.5 indicates that the model is still quite capable of replicating rather reasonably the population estimates of McEvedy and Jones (1978) and Kremer (1993) for the 10000 – 500 BCE period:

Diagram 2.5.   Predicted and Observed Dynamics
of the World Population Growth,
in millions (10000 – 500 BCE)

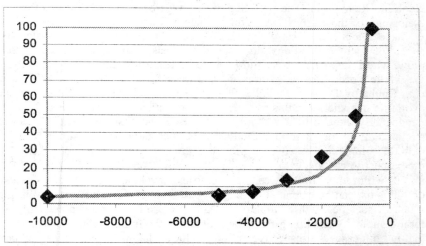

NOTE: The solid grey curve has been generated by the model; black markers correspond to the estimates of world population by McEvedy and Jones (1978) and Kremer (1993).

The correlation between the predicted and observed values for this simulation looks as follows: $R = 0.982$, $R^2 = 0.964$, $p = 0.0001$. Note that though this correlation for 10000 – 500 BCE remains rather high, it is substantially weaker[11] than the one observed above for the 500 BCE – 1962 CE and, especially, 1650–1962 CE (in fact this is visible quite clearly even without special statistical analysis in Diagrams 2.1, 2.3, and 2.5). On the one hand, this result could hardly be regarded as surprising, because it appears evident that in 10000 – 500 BCE the World System was much less tightly integrated than in 500 BCE – 1962 CE (let alone in 1650–1962 CE). What seems more remarkable is that for 10000 – 500 BCE the best fit is achieved with a substantially different value of the coefficient c, which appears to indicate that the World System development

---

[11] Note, however, that even for 10000 – 500 BCE our hyperbolic growth model still demonstrates a much higher fit with the observed data than, for example, the best-fit exponential model ($R^2 = 0.737$, $p = 0.0003$).

pattern in the pre-500 BCE epoch was substantially different from the one observed in the 500 BCE – 1962 CE era, and thus implies a radical transformation of the World System in the 1st millennium BCE..

We believe that among other things the compact macromodel analysis seems to suggest a rather novel approach to World System analysis. The hyperbolic trend observed for world population growth after 10000 BCE mostly appears to be a product of the growth of the World System, which seems to have originated in West Asia around that time in direct connection with the Neolithic Revolution. The presence of the hyperbolic trend indicates that the major part of the entity in question had some systemic unity, and, we believe we have evidence for this unity. Indeed, we have evidence for the systematic spread of major innovations (domesticated cereals, cattle, sheep, goats, horses, plow, wheel, copper, bronze, and later iron technology, and so on) throughout the whole North African – Eurasian Oikumene for a few millennia BCE (see, e.g., Chubarov 1991; Diamond 1999 etc.). As a result, already at this time the evolution of societies in this part of the world cannot be regarded as truly independent. By the end of the 1st millennium BCE we observe a belt of cultures stretching from the Atlantic to the Pacific with an astonishingly similar level of cultural complexity based on agriculture involving production of wheat and other specific cereals, cattle, sheep, goats, plow, iron metallurgy, professional armies with rather similar weapons, cavalries, developed bureaucracies and so on – this list can be extended for pages. A few millennia before we would find a belt of societies with a similarly strikingly close level and character of cultural complexity stretching from the Balkans to the Indus Valley borders (note that in both cases the respective entities included the major part of the contemporary world population). We would interpret this as tangible results of the World System functioning. The alternative explanations would involve a sort of miraculous scenario – that cultures with strikingly similar levels and character of complexity somehow developed independently from each other in a very large but continuous zone, whereas nothing like them appeared in other parts of the world, which were not parts of the World System. We find such an alternative explanation highly implausible.

It could be suggested that within a new approach the main emphasis would be moved to the generation and diffusion of innovations. If a society borrows systematically important technological innovations, its evolution already cannot be considered as really independent, but should rather be considered as a part of a larger evolving entity, within which such innovations are systematically produced and diffused. The main idea of the world-system approach was to find the evolving unit. The basic idea was that it is impossible to account for the evolution of a single society without taking into consideration that it was a part of a larger whole. However, traditional world-system analysis concentrated on bulk-good movements, and core – periphery exploitation, thoroughly neglecting the above-mentioned dimension. However, the information network turns out to be the oldest mechanism of the World System integration, and remained extremely important throughout its whole history, remaining important up to the present. It seems to be even more important than the core – periphery exploitation (for example, without taking this mechanism into consideration it appears impossible to account for such things as the demographic explosion in the 20th century, whose proximate cause was the dramatic decline of mortality, but whose main ultimate cause was the diffusion of innovations produced almost exclusively within the World System core). This also suggests a redefinition of the World System (WS) core. The core is not the WS zone, which exploits other zones, but rather the WS core is the zone with the highest innovation donor/recipient (D/R) ratio, the principal innovation donor.[12]

---

[12] Earlier we regarded an "information network" as a sufficient condition to consider the entity covered by it as a "world-system". However, some examples seem to be rather telling in this respect. *E.g.*, Gudmund Hatt (1949: 104) found evidence on not fewer than 60 Japanese ships accidentally brought by the Kurosio and North Pacific currents to the New World coast between 1617 and 1876. Against this background it appears remarkable that the "Japanese [mythology] hardly contains any motifs that are not found in America (which was noticed by Levi-Strauss long ago)" (Berezkin 2002: 290–1). Already this fact does not make it possible to exclude entirely the possibility of some information finding its way to the New World from the Old World in the pre-Columbian era, information that could even influence the evolution of some Amerindian mythologies. However, we do not think this is sufficient to consider the New World as a part of the pre-Columbian World System. The Japanese might have even told Amerindians about such wonderful animals as horses, or cows (and some scholars even claim that a few pre-Columbian Amerindian images depict Old World animals [von Heine-Geldern 1964; Kazankov 2006]); the Japanese fishermen might even have had some idea of say, horse breeding. But all such information would have been entirely useless without some specific matter – actual horses or cows. Hence, now we would denote respective "system-creating" networks as "innovation diffusion networks" rather than just "information networks".

Chapter 3

A Compact Macromodel of
World Economic and Demographic Growth

Before proposing this model, it appears necessary to consider in more detail the model developed by Michael Kremer (1993).

Kremer assumes that overall output produced by the world economy equals

$$G = rTN^{\alpha}V^{1-\alpha},$$

where G is output, T is the level of technology, N is population, V is land, r and α ($0 < \alpha < 1$) are parameters. Actually Kremer uses a variant of the Cobb-Douglas production function. Kremer further qualifies that variable V is normalized to one. The resultant equation for output is:

$$G = rTN^{\alpha},\tag{3.1}$$

where r and α are constants.

Further Kremer uses the Malthusian assumption, formulating it in the following way: "In this simplified model I assume that population adjusts instantaneously to $\overline{N}$ " (Kremer 1993: 685). Value $\overline{N}$ in this model corresponds to population size, at which it produces equilibrium level of per capita income $\overline{g}$, whereas "population increases above some steady state equilibrium level of per capita income, $\overline{g}$, and decreases below it" (Kremer 1993: 685).

Thus, the equilibrium level of population $\overline{N}$ is

$$\overline{N} = \left(\frac{\overline{g}}{T}\right)^{\frac{1}{\alpha-1}}.\tag{3.2}$$

Hence, the equation for population size is not actually dynamic. In Kremer's model the dynamic element is introduced by a supplementary equation for technological growth. Kremer uses the following assumption of the Endogenous Technological Growth theory, which we have already used above for the development of the first compact macromodel (Kuznets 1960; Grossman and

Helpman 1991; Aghion and Howitt 1992, 1998; Simon 1977, 1981, 2000; Komlos and Nefedov 2002; Jones 1995, 2003, 2005 *etc.*):

"High population spurs technological change because it increases the number of potential inventors...[1]. All else equal, each person's chance of inventing something is independent of population. Thus, in a larger population there will be proportionally more people lucky or smart enough to come up with new ideas" (Kremer 1993: 685); thus, "the growth rate of technology is proportional to total population" (Kremer 1993: 682). (3.3)

Since this supposition was first proposed by Simon Kuznets (1960), we shall denote the respective type of dynamics as "Kuznetsian"; and we shall denote as "Malthusian-Kuznetsian" those systems where "Kuznetsian" population-technological dynamics is combined with "Malthusian" demographics.

The Kuznetsian assumption is expressed mathematically by Kremer in the following way:

$$\frac{dT}{dt} : T = bN ,$$ (3.4)

where b is average innovating productivity per person.

Note that this implies that the dynamics of absolute technological growth rate can be described by the following equation:

$$\frac{dT}{dt} = bNT .$$ (3.5)

Kremer further combines the research and population determination equations in the following way:

"Since population is limited by technology, the growth rate of population is proportional to the growth rate of technology. Since the growth rate of technology is proportional to the level of population, the growth rate of population must also be proportional to the level of population. To see this formally, take the logarithm of the population determination equation, [(3.2)], and differentiate with respect to time:

$$\frac{dN}{dt} : N = \frac{1}{1-\alpha}(\frac{dT}{dt} : T) .$$

Substitute in the expression for the growth rate of technology from [(3.4)], to obtain

---

[1] "This implication flows naturally from the nonrivalry of technology... The cost of inventing a new technology is independent of the number of people who use it. Thus, holding constant the share of resources devoted to research, an increase in population leads to an increase in technological change" (Kremer 1993: 681).

$$\frac{dN}{dt} : N = \frac{g}{1-\alpha} N \text{ " (Kremer 1993: 686).} \qquad (3.6)$$

Note that multiplying both parts of equation (3.6) by N we get

$$\frac{dN}{dt} = aN^2 , \qquad (2.4')$$

where a equals

$$a = \frac{g}{1-\alpha} .$$

Of course, the same equation can be also written as

$$\frac{dN}{dt} = \frac{N^2}{C} , \qquad (2.4)$$

where C equals

$$C = \frac{1-\alpha}{g} .$$

Thus, Kremer's model produces precisely the same dynamics as the ones of von Foerster and Kapitza (and, consequently, it has just the same phenomenal fit with the observed data). However, it also provides a very convincing explanation WHY throughout most of the human history the absolute world population growth rate tended to be proportional to N^2. Within both models the growth of population from, say, 10 million to 100 million will result in the growth of dN/dt 100 times. However, von Foerster and Kapitza failed to explain convincingly why dN/dt tended to be proportional to N^2. Kremer's model explains this in what seems to us a rather convincing way (though Kremer himself does not appear to have spelled this out in a sufficiently clear way). The point is that the growth of the world population from 10 to 100 million implies that the human technology also grew approximately 10 times (as it turns out to be able to support a ten times larger population). On the other hand, the growth of population 10 times also implies 10-fold growth of the number of potential inventors, and, hence, 10-fold increase in the relative technological growth rate. Hence, the absolute technological growth will grow 10 x 10 = 100 times (in accordance to equation (3.5)). And as N tends to the technologically determined carrying capacity ceiling, we have all grounds to expect that dN/dt will also grow just 100 times.

Though Kremer's model provides a virtual explanation of how the World System's techno-economic development, in connection with demographic dynamics, could lead to hyperbolic population growth, Kremer did not specify his model to such an extent that it could also describe the economic development of the World System and that such a description could be tested empirically.[2] Nevertheless, it appears possible to propose a very simple mathematical model describing both the demographic and economic development of the World System up to 1973 using the same assumptions as those employed by Kremer.

Kremer's analysis suggests the following relationship between per capita GDP and population growth rate (see Diagram 3.1):

Diagram 3.1. Relationship between per capita GDP and Population Growth Rate according to Kremer (1993)

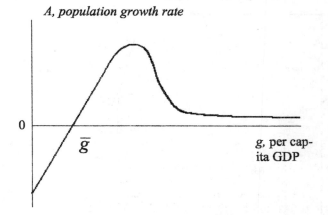

This suggests that in the lower range of per capita GDP the influence of this variable on the dynamics of population growth can be described with the following equation:

$$\frac{dN}{dt} = aSN, \qquad (3.7)$$

where S is surplus, which is produced per person over the amount (m), which is minimally necessary to reproduce the population with a zero growth rate in a Malthusian system (thus, $S = g - m$, where g denotes per capita GDP).

---

[2] In fact, such an operationalization did not make sense at the time when Kremer's article was submitted for publication, as the long term empirical data on the world GDP dynamics were not simply available at that moment.

Note that this model generates predictions that can be tested empirically.
For example, the model predicts that relative world population growth
($r_N = \dfrac{dN}{dt} : N$) should be lineally proportional to the world per capita surplus
production:

$$r_N = aS \; . \tag{3.8}$$

The empirical test of this hypothesis has supported it. The respective correlation has turned out to be in the predicted direction, very strong ($R = 0.961$), and
significant beyond any doubt ($p = 0.00004$) (see Diagram 3.2):

Diagram 3.2.   Correlation between the per capita surplus production
and world population growth rates for 1–1973 CE
(scatterplot with fitted regression line)

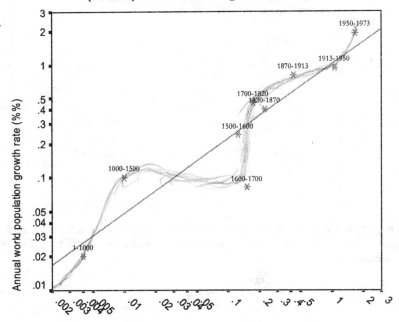

Per capita surplus production (thousands of 1990 int.dollars,PPP)

NOTES: $R = 0.961$, $p = 0.00004$. Data source – Maddison 2001; Maddison's estimate of the world
per capita GDP for 1000 CE has been corrected on the basis of Meliantsev (1996: 55–97). S values
were calculated on the basis of m estimated as 440 international 1990 dollars in purchasing power
parity (PPP); for the justification of this estimate see Korotayev, Malkov, and Khaltourina
2005: 43–51.

The mechanisms of this relationship are perfectly evident. In the range $440–3500[3] the per capita GDP growth leads to very substantial improvements in nutrition, health care, sanitation *etc.* resulting in a precipitous decline of death rates (see, *e.g.*, Diagram 3.3):

Diagram 3.3.   Correlation between per capita GDP and death rate for countries of the world in 1975

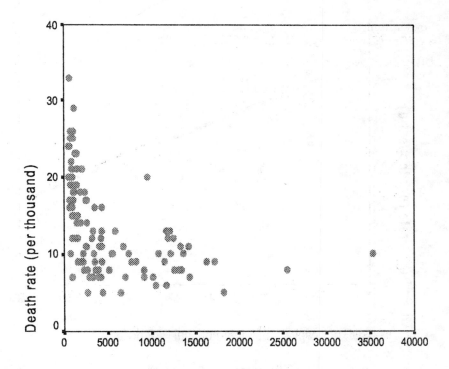

NOTE: data sources – Maddison 2001 (for per capita GDP), World Bank 2005 (for death rate).

For example, for 1960 the correlation between per capita GDP and death rate for $440–3500 range reaches – 0.634 (p = 0.0000000001) (see Diagram 3.4):

---

[3] Here and throughout the GDP is measured in 1990 international purchasing power parity dollars after Maddison (2001) if not stated otherwise.

Diagram 3.4.   Correlation between per capita GDP and death rate
for countries of the world in 1960 (for $440–3500 range)

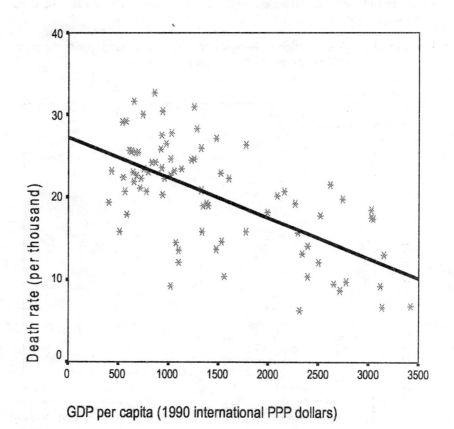

GDP per capita (1990 international PPP dollars)

NOTE: $R = -0.634$, $p = 0.0000000001$. Data sources – Maddison 2001 (for per capita GDP), World Bank 2005 (for death rate).

Note that during the earliest stages of demographic transition (corresponding just to the range in question) the decline of the death rates is not accompanied by a corresponding decline of the birth rates (*e.g.*, Chesnais 1992); in fact, they can even grow (see, *e.g.*, Diagram 3.5).

Diagram 3.5.   Economic and demographic dynamics in Sierra Leone, 1960–1970

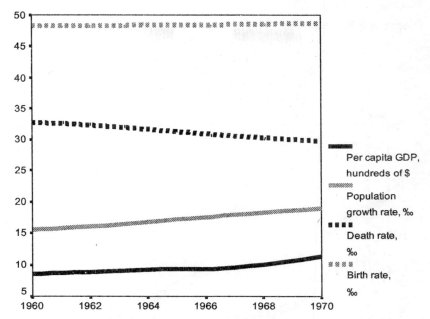

NOTE: Data sources – Maddison 2001 (for per capita GDP), World Bank 2005 (for demographic variables).

Indeed, say a decline of the death rates from, *e.g.*, 50 to 25‰ implies the growth of life expectancies from 20 to 40 years, whereas a woman living 40 years can bear many more babies than when she dies at the age of 20. In many countries the growth of the fertility rates in the range in question was also connected with the reduction of spacing between births, due to such modernization-produced changes as an abandonment of traditional postpartum sex taboos, or due to a reduction of lactation periods (given the growing availability of foods that can serve as substitutes for maternal milk). Against this background the radical decline of the death rates at the earliest stages of demographic transition is accompanied by as a radical increase of the population growth rates.

Note that equation (3.7) is not valid for the GDP per capita range > $3500. In this "post-Malthusian" range the death rate reaches bottom levels and then starts slightly growing due to the population aging, whereas the growth of such variables as education (and especially female education), level of social security subsystem development, growing availability of more and more sophisticated family planning techniques *etc.* leads to a sharp decline of birth rates (see, *e.g.*, Hollingsworth 1996, Bongaarts 2003, Korotayev, Malkov, and Khaltourina 2005). As a result in this range the further growth of per capita GDP leads not to the increase of the population growth rates, but to their substantial decrease (see Diagram 3.6):

Diagram 3.6.   Relationships between per capita GDP
(1990 international PPP dollars, X-axis),
Death Rates (‰, Y-axis), Birth Rates (‰, Y-axis),
and Population Growth Rates[4] (‰, Y-axis), nations
with per capita GDP > $3500, 1975,
scatterplot with fitted Lowess lines

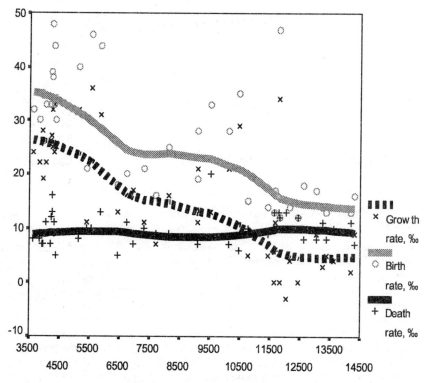

NOTE: Data sources – Maddison 2001 (for per capita GDP), World Bank 2005 (for the other data).

---

[4] Internal ("natural") population growth rate calculated as birth rate minus death rate. We used this variable instead of standard growth rate, as the latter takes into account the influence of emigration and immigration processes, which notwithstanding all their importance are not relevant for the subject of this chapter, because though they could affect in a most significant way the population growth rates of particular countries, they do not affect the world population growth.

This pattern is even more pronounced for the world countries of 2001, as between 1975 and 2001 the number of countries that had moved out of the first phase of demographic transition to the "post-Malthusian world" substantially increased (see Diagram 3.7):

Diagram 3.7.   Relationships between per capita GDP
(2001 PPP USD, X-axis), Death Rates (‰, Y-axis),
Birth Rates (‰, Y-axis), and Population Growth
Rates (‰, Y-axis), nations with per capita
GDP > $3000, 2001, scatterplot with fitted Lowess lines

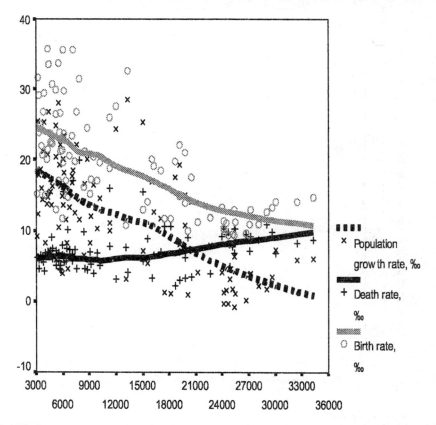

NOTE: Data source – World Bank 2005. Omitting the former Communist countries of Europe, which are characterized by a very specific pattern of demographic growth (or, in fact, to be more exact, demographic decline – see, *e.g.*, Korotayev, Malkov, and Khaltourina 2005: 302–29).

It is also highly remarkable that as soon as the world per capita GDP (g) approached $3000 and exceeded this (thus, with $S \sim$ $2500), the positive correlation between S and r first dropped to zero (see Diagram 3.8); beyond $S = 3300$ ($g \sim 3700$) it becomes strongly negative (see Diagram 3.9), whereas in the range of $S > 4800$ ($g > 5200$) this negative correlation becomes almost perfect (see Diagram 3.10):

Diagram. 3.8. Correlation between the per capita surplus production and world population growth rates for the range $2400 < S < $3500 (scatterplot with fitted regression line)

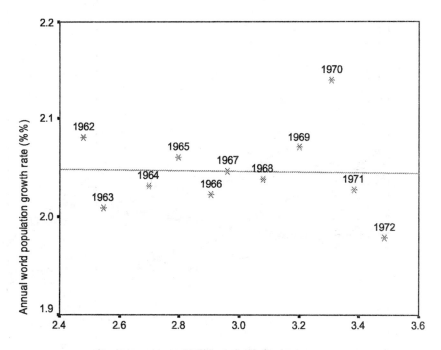

Per capita surplus production (thousands of 1990 int.dollars,PPP)

NOTES: $R = -0.028$, $p = 0.936$. Data source – Maddison 2001.

Diagram 3.9.   Correlation between the per capita surplus production
and world population growth rates for *S* > $4800
(scatterplot with fitted regression line)

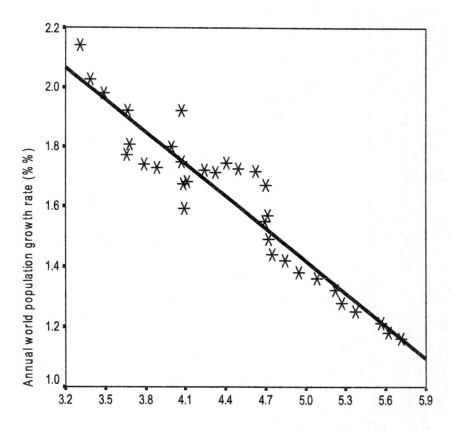

Per capita surplus production (thousands of 1990 int.dollars,PPP)

NOTES: $R = -0.946$, $p = 0.0000000000000003$. Data sources – Maddison 2001 (for the world per capita GDP, 1970–1998 and the world population growth rates, 1970–1988); World Bank 2005 (for the world per capita GDP, 1999–2002); United Nations 2005 (for the world population growth rates, 1989–2002).

Diagram 3.10. Correlation between the per capita surplus production
and world population growth rates for $S > \$4800$
(scatterplot with fitted regression line)

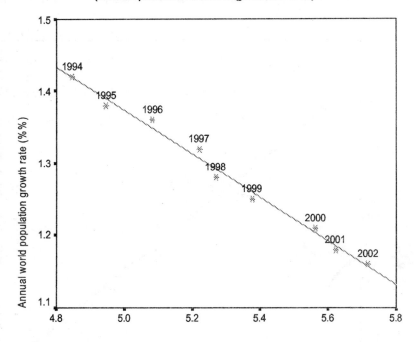

Per capita surplus production (thousands of 1990 int.dollars,PPP)

NO
TES: $R = -0.995$, $p = 0.00000004$. Data sources – Maddison 2001 (for the world per capita GDP, 1994–1998); World Bank 2005 (for the world per capita GDP, 1999–2002); United Nations 2005 (for the world population growth rates).

Thus, to describe the relationships between economic and demographic growth in the "post-Malthusian" GDP per capita range of $> \$3000$, equation (3.7) should be modified, which is quite possible, but which goes beyond the scope of this chapter aimed at the description of economic and demographic macro-dynamics of the "Malthusian" period of human history; this and will be done in the subsequent chapters.

As was already noted by Kremer (1993: 694), in conjunction with equation (3.1) an equation of type (3.7) "in the absence of technological change [that is if $T = $ const] reduces to a purely Malthusian system, and produces behavior similar to the logistic curve biologists use to describe animal populations facing fixed resources" (actually, we would add to Kremer's biologists those social scientists who model pre-industrial demographic cycles – see, *e.g.*, Usher 1989;

Chu and Lee 1994; Nefedov 2002, 2004; Malkov 2002, 2003, 2004; Malkov and Sergeev 2002, 2004; Malkov, Selunskaja, and Sergeev 2005; Turchin 2003; Korotayev, Malkov, and Khaltourina 2005).

Note that with a constant relative technological growth rate ($\frac{\dot{T}}{T} = r_T = const$) within this model (combining equations (3.1) and (3.7)) we will have both constant relative population growth rate ($\frac{\dot{N}}{N} = r_N = const$, and thus the population will grow exponentially) and constant S. Note also that the higher value of r_T we take, the higher value of constant S we get.

Let us show this formally.

Take the following system:

$$G = gTN^{\alpha} \tag{3.1}$$

$$\frac{dN}{dt} = aSN \tag{3.7}$$

$$\frac{dT}{dt} = cT, \tag{3.9}$$

where $S = \frac{G}{N} - m$.

Equation (3.9) evidently gives $T = T_0 e^{ct}$. Thus, $G = gT_0 e^{ct} N^{\alpha}$, and consequently

$$\frac{dN}{dt} = a\left(\frac{gT_0 e^{ct} N^{\alpha}}{N} - m \right)N = agT_0 e^{ct} N^{\alpha} - amN.$$

This is known as a Bernoulli differential equation: $\frac{dy}{dx} = f(x)y + g(x)y^{\alpha}$, which has the following solution:

$$y^{1-\alpha} = Ce^{F(x)} + (1-\alpha)e^{F(x)} \int e^{-F(x)} g(x)dx,$$

where $F(x) = (1-\alpha) \int f(x)dx$, and C is constant.

In the case considered above, we have

$$N^{1-\alpha} = Ce^{F(t)} + \left(1-\alpha\right)e^{F(t)}\int e^{-F(t)}agT_0 e^{ct}dt,$$

where $F(t) = \left(1-\alpha\right)\int\left(-am\right)dt = \left(\alpha-1\right)amt$.

So $N^{1-\alpha} = Ce^{(\alpha-1)amt} + \left(1-\alpha\right)agT_0 e^{(\alpha-1)amt}\int e^{-(\alpha-1)amt}e^{ct}dt$

$$N^{1-\alpha} = e^{-(1-\alpha)amt}\left(C + \left(1-\alpha\right)agT_0\int e^{(c+(1-\alpha)am)t}dt\right)$$

$$N^{1-\alpha} = e^{-(1-\alpha)amt}\left(C + \frac{\left(1-\alpha\right)agT_0}{c+\left(1-\alpha\right)am}e^{(c+(1-\alpha)am)t}\right)$$

This result causes the following equation for S:

$$S = \frac{gT_0 e^{ct}N^{\alpha}}{N} - m = gT_0 e^{ct}N^{\alpha-1} - m = \frac{gT_0 e^{(c+(1-\alpha)am)t}}{C + \dfrac{\left(1-\alpha\right)agT_0}{c+\left(1-\alpha\right)am}e^{(c+(1-\alpha)am)t}} - m;$$

$$S = \frac{1}{\dfrac{C}{gT_0}e^{-(c+(1-\alpha)am)t} + \dfrac{\left(1-\alpha\right)a}{c+\left(1-\alpha\right)am}} - m.$$

Since $c > 0$ and $\left(1-\alpha\right) > 0$, it is clear that $c + \left(1-\alpha\right)am > 0$.

Consequently $e^{-(c+(1-\alpha)am)t} \to 0$ as $t \to \infty$.

This means that $S \xrightarrow[t\to\infty]{} \dfrac{c+\left(1-\alpha\right)am}{\left(1-\alpha\right)a} - m$, or finally

$$S \to \frac{c}{\left(1-\alpha\right)a}, \text{ as } t \to \infty.$$

Note that coefficient c in equation (3.9) is nothing else but just the relative technological growth rate ($r_T = dT/dt : T$). Thus within the system (3.1)-(3.7)-(3.9), with a constant relative technological growth rate ($r_T = c$), the per capita surplus (S) would also tend to some constant, and the higher value of relative technological growth rate ($c = r_T$) we take, the higher value of constant S we get at the end.

This, of course, suggests that in the growing "Malthusian" systems S could be regarded as a rather sensitive indicator of the speed of technological growth. Indeed, within Malthusian systems in the absence of technological growth the demographic growth will lead to S tending to 0, whereas a long-term systematic production of S will be only possible with systematic technological growth.[5]

---

[5] It might make sense to stress that it is not coincidental that we are speaking here just about the long-term perspective, as in a shorter-term perspective it would be necessary to take into account that within the actual Malthusian systems S was also produced quite regularly at the recovery

Now replace $\dfrac{\dot{T}}{T} = r_T = const$ with Kremer's technological growth equation (3.5) and analyze the resultant model:

$$G = aTN^{\alpha} ,$$ (3.1)

$$\frac{dN}{dt} = bSN ,$$ (3.7)

$$\frac{dT}{dt} = cNT .$$ (3.5)

Within this model, quite predictably, S can be approximated as kr_T. On the other hand, within this model, by definition, r_T is directly proportional to N. Thus, the model generates an altogether not so self-evident (one could say even a bit unlikely) prediction – that throughout the "Malthusian-Kuznetsian" part of the human history the world per capita surplus production must have tended to be directly proportional to the world population size. This hypothesis, of course, deserves to be empirically tested. In fact, our tests have supported it.

Our test for the whole part of human history for which we have empirical estimates for both the world population and the world GDP (that is for 1–2002 CE[6]) has produced the following results: $R^2 = 0.98$, $p < 10^{-16}$, whereas for the period with the most pronounced "Malthusian-Kuznetsian" dynamics (1820–1958) the positive correlation between the two variables is almost perfect (see Diagram 3.11):

---

phases of pre-Industrial political-demographic cycles (following political-demographic collapses as a result of which the surviving population found itself abundantly provided with resources). However, after the recovery phases the continuing production of significant amounts of S (and, hence, the continuing significant population growth) was only possible against the background of significant technological growth (see, _e.g._, Korotayev, Malkov, Khaltourina 2005: 160–228). Note also that S produced at the initial (recovery) phases of political-demographic cycles in no way can explain the millennial trend towards the growth of S which was observed for many centuries before most of the world population moved to the second phase of demographic transition (_e.g._, Maddison 2001) and that appears to have been produced just by the accelerating technological growth.

[6] Data sources – Maddison 2001 (world population and GDP, 1–1998 CE), World Bank 2005 (world GDP, 1999–2002), United Nations 2005 (world population, 1999–2002).

Diagram 3.11. Correlation between world population
and per capita surplus production (1820–1958)

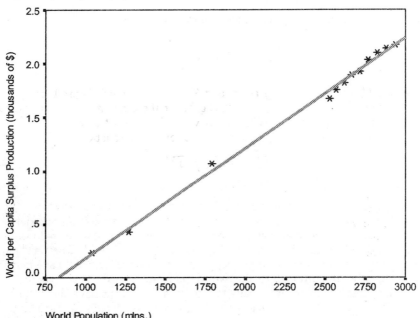

World Population (mins.)

NOTE: $R^2 > 0.996$, $p < 10^{-12}$.

Note that as within a Malthusian-Kuznetsian system S can be approximated as
kN, equation (3.7) may be approximated as $dN/dt \sim k_1N^2$ (2.4'), or, of course, as
$dN/dt \sim N^2 / C$ (2.4); thus, Kapitza's equation (2.4) turns out to be a by-product
of the model under consideration.

Thus, we arrive at the following:

$$S \sim k_1 r_T,$$

$$r_T = k_2 N.$$

Hence,

$$dS/dt \sim kr_T/dt = k_3 dN/dt.$$

This implies that for the "Malthusian-Kuznetsian" part of human history dS/dt
can be approximates as $k_4 dN/dt$.

On the other hand, as dN/dt in the original model equals aSN, this, of
course, suggests that for the respective part of the human history both the eco-

nomic and demographic World System dynamics may be approximated by the following unlikely simple mathematical model:[7]

$$\frac{dN}{dt} = aSN \quad , \tag{3.7}$$

$$\frac{dS}{dt} = bNS \quad , \tag{3.10}$$

where N is the world population, and S is surplus, which is produced per person with the given level of technology over the amount, which is minimally necessary to reproduce the population with a zero growth rate.

The world GDP is computed using the following equation:

$$G = mN + SN \quad , \tag{3.11}$$

where m denotes the amount of per capita GDP, which is minimally necessary to reproduce the population with a zero growth rate, and S denotes "surplus" produced per capita over m at the given level of the world-system techno-economic development.

Note that this model does not contain any variables for which we do not have empirical data (at least for 1–1973) and, thus, a full empirical test for this model turns out to be perfectly possible.[8]

Incidentally, this model implies that the absolute rate of the world population growth (dN/dt) should have been roughly proportional to the absolute rate of the increase in the world per capita surplus production (dS/dt), and, thus (assuming the value of necessary product to be constant), to the absolute rate of the world per capita GDP growth, with which dS/dt will be measured thereafter. Note that among other things this could help us to determine the proportion between coefficients a and b.

Thus, if the model suggested by us has some correspondence to reality, one has grounds to expect that in the "Malthusian-Kuznetsian" period of the human history the absolute world population growth rate (dN/dt) was directly proportional to the absolute growth rate of the world per capita surplus production

---

[7] Note that this model only describes the Malthusian-Kuznetsian World System in a dynamically balanced state (when the observed world population is in a balanced correspondence with the observed technological level). To describe the situations with N disproportionally low or high for the given level of technology (and, hence, disproportionally high or low S) one would need, of course, the unapproximated version of the model ((3.1) – (3.7) – (3.5)). Note, that in such cases N will either grow, or decline up to the dynamic equilibrium level, after which the developmental trajectory will follow the line described by the (3.7) – (3.10) model.

[8] This refers particularly to the long-range data on the level of world technological development (T), which do not appear to be available now.

(dS/dt). The correlation between these two variables looks as follows (see Diagram 3.12):

Diagram 3.12. Correlation between World Average Annual Absolute Growth Rate of Per Capita Surplus Production (S, 1990 PPP international dollars) and Average Annual Absolute World Population (N) Growth Rate (1 – 1973 CE), scatterplot in logarithmic scale with a regression line

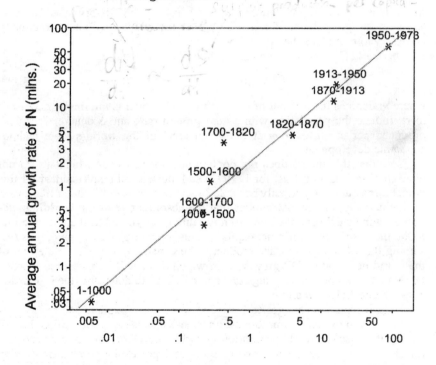

Average annual growth rate of S (1990 international $$)

NOTE: Data source – Maddison 2001; Maddison's estimates of the world per capita GDP for 1000 CE has been corrected on the basis of Meliantsev (1996: 55–97).

Regression analysis of this dataset has given the following results (see Table 3.1):

Table 3.1. Correlation between World Average Annual Absolute Growth Rate of Per Capita Surplus Production (*S*, 1990 PPP international dollars) and Average Annual Absolute World Population (*N*) Growth Rate (1 – 1950 CE), (regression analysis)

Model	Unstandardized Coefficients		Standardized Coefficients	t	Sig.
	B	Std. Error	Beta		
(Constant)	0.820	0.935		0.876	0.414
World Average Annual Absolute Growth Rate of Per Capita Surplus Production (1990 PPP international dollars / year)	0.981	0.118	0.959	8.315	<0.001
Dependent variable: Average Annual Absolute World Population Growth Rate (mlns. / year)					

$R = 0.96$, $R^2 = 0.92$

Note that the constant in this case is very small within the data scale, statistically insignificant, and lies within the standard error from 0, which makes it possible to equate it with 0. In this case regression analysis gives the following results (see Table 3.2):

Table 3.2. Correlation between World Average Annual Absolute Growth Rate of Per Capita Surplus Production (*S*, 1990 PPP international dollars) and Average Annual Absolute World Population (*N*) Growth Rate (1 – 1950 CE), (regression analysis, not including constant in equation)

Model	Unstandardized Coefficients		Standardized Coefficients	t	Sig.
	B	Std. Error	Beta		
World Average Annual Absolute Growth Rate of Per Capita Surplus Production (1990 PPP international dollars / year)	1.04	0.095	0.972	10.94	<0.001
Dependent variable: Average Annual Absolute World Population Growth Rate (mlns. / year)					

$R = 0.97$, $R^2 = 0.945$

Thus, just as implied by our second model, in the "Malthusian" period of human history we do observe a strong linear relationship between the annual absolute world population growth rates (dN/dt) and the annual absolute growth rates of per capita surplus production (dS/dt). This relationship can be described mathematically with the following equation:

$$\frac{dN}{dt} = 1.04 \, \frac{dS}{dt} \, ,$$

where N is the world population (in millions), and S is surplus (in 1990 PPP international dollars), which is produced per person with the given level of technology over the amount, which is minimally necessary to reproduce the population with a zero growth rate.

Note that according to model (3.7, 3.10),

$$\frac{dN}{dt} = \frac{a}{b} \, \frac{dS}{dt} \, .$$

Thus, it becomes possible to express coefficient b through coefficient a:

$$\frac{a}{b} = 1.04 \, ,$$

consequently:

$$b = \frac{a}{1.04} = 0.96 \, a \, .$$

As a result, for the period under consideration it appears possible to simplify the second compact macromodel, leaving in it just one free coefficient:

$$\frac{dN}{dt} = aSN \, , \tag{3.7}$$

$$\frac{dS}{dt} = 0.96 \, aNS \, , \tag{3.12}$$

With our two-equation model we start the simulation in the year 1 CE and do annual iterations with difference equations derived from the differential ones:

$$N_{i+1} = N_i + aS_iN_i,$$
$$S_{i+1} = S_i + 0.96aN_iS_i \, .$$

The world GDP is calculated using equation (3.11).

We choose the following values of the constants and initial conditions in accordance with historical estimates of Maddison (2001): $N_0 = 230.82$ (in millions); $a = 0.000011383$; $S_0 = 4.225$ (in International 1990 PPP dollars).[9]

The outcome of the simulation, presented in Diagram 3.13 indicates that the compact macromodel in question is actually capable of replicating quite reasonably the world GDP estimates of Maddison (2001):

Diagram 3.13. Predicted and Observed Dynamics
of the World GDP Growth, in billions of 1990 PPP
international dollars (1 – 1973 CE)

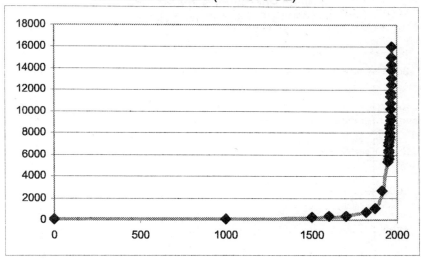

NOTE: The solid grey curve has been generated by the model; black markers correspond to the estimates of world GDP by Maddison (2001).

---

[9] The value of S_0 was calculated with equation $S = G/N - m$ on the basis of Maddison's (2001) estimates for the year 1 CE. He estimates the world population in this year as 230.82 million, the world GDP as \$102.536 billion (in 1990 PPP international dollars), and hence, the world per capita GDP production as \$444.225 Maddison estimates the subsistence level per capita annual GDP production as \$400 (2001: 260, 264). However, already by 1 CE most population of the world lived in rather complex societies, where the population reproduction even at zero level still required considerable production over subsistence level to maintain various infrastructures (transportation, legal, security, administrative and other subsystems *etc.*), without which even the simple reproduction of complex societies is impossible almost by definition. Note that the fall of per capita production in complex agrarian societies to subsistence level tended to lead to state breakdowns and demographic collapses (see, *e.g.*, Turchin 2003; Nefedov 2004; Malkov, Selunskaja, and Sergeev 2005; Korotayev, Malkov, and Khaltourina 2005). The per capita production to support the above mentioned infrastructures could hardly be lower than 10% of the subsistence level – that is close to Maddison's (2001: 259–60) estimates, which makes it possible to estimate the value of m as \$440, and hence, the value of S_0 as \$4.225.

The correlation between the predicted and observed values for this simulation looks as follows: $R > 0.999$; $R^2 = 0.9986$; $p \ll 0.0001$. For the world population these characteristics are also very high: $R = 0.996$; $R^2 = 0.992$; $p \ll 0.0001$.

According both to our model and the observed data up to the early 1970s we deal with the hyperbolic growth of not only the world population (N), but also per capita surplus production (S) (see Diagram 3.14):

Diagram 3.14. Hyperbolic Growth
of World Per Capita Surplus Production,
in 1990 PPP international dollars
(1 – 1973 CE)

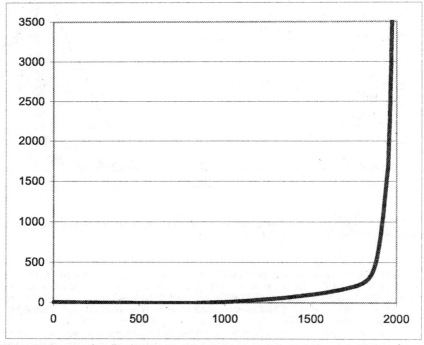

NOTE: Data source – Maddison 2001; Maddison's estimates of the world per capita GDP for 1000 CE has been corrected on the basis of Meliantsev (1996: 55–97).

Note that even if S had not been growing, remaining constant, the world GDP would have been growing hyperbolically anyway through the hyperbolic growth of the world population only. However, the hyperbolic growth of S observed during this period of the human history led to the fact that the world population correlated with the world GDP not lineally, but quadratically (see Diagram 3.15):

Diagram 3.15.　Correlation between World Population
　　　　　　　　and World GDP (1 – 1973 CE)

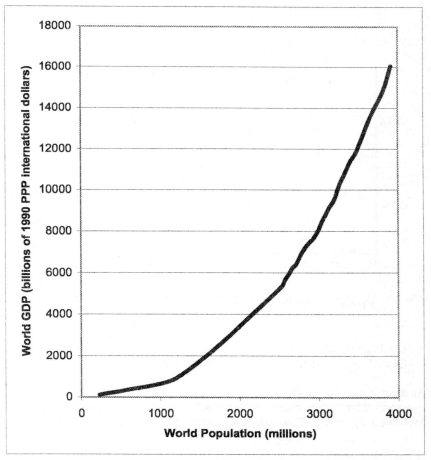

NOTE: Data source – Maddison 2001; Maddison's estimates of the world per capita GDP for 1000 CE has been corrected on the basis of Meliantsev (1996: 55–97).

Indeed, the regression analysis we have performed has shown here an almost perfect ($R^2 = 0.998$) fit just with the quadratic model (see Diagram 3.16):

Diagram 3.16. Correlation between Dynamics of the World Population
and GDP Growth (1 – 1973 CE): curve estimations

World GDP (billions of international $)

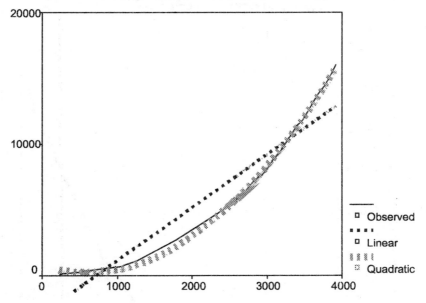

World population (millions)

LINEAR REGRESSION: $R^2 = 0.876, p < 0.001$
QUADRATIC REGRESSION: $R^2 = 0.998, p < 0.001$

As a result the overall dynamics of the world's GDP up to 1973 was not even
hyperbolic, but rather quadratic-hyperbolic, leaving far behind the impressive
hyperbolic dynamics of the world population growth (see Diagram 3.17):

Diagram 3.17. The World GDP Growth from 1 CE up to the early 1970s
(in billions of 1990 PPP international dollars)

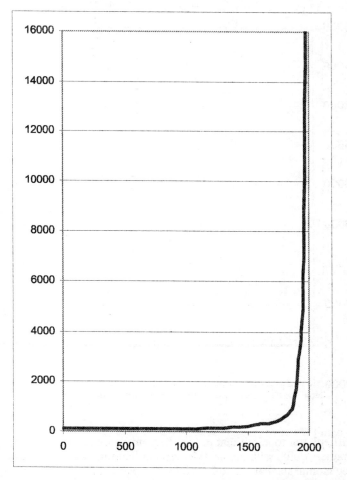

NOTE: Data source – Maddison 2001; Maddison's estimates of the world per capita GDP for 1000 CE has been corrected on the basis of Meliantsev (1996: 55–97).

The world GDP growth dynamics would look especially impressive if we take into account the quite plausible estimates of this variable change before 1 CE produced by DeLong (1998), see Diagram 3.18:

Diagram 3.18. World GDP Growth from 25000 BCE
up to the early 1970s
(in billions of 1990 PPP international dollars)

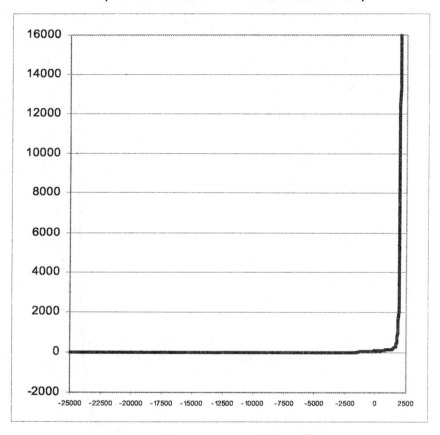

It is difficult not to admit that in this diagram human economic history appears to be rather "dull", with the pre-Modern era looking as a period of almost complete economic stagnation, followed by explosive modern economic growth. In reality the latter just does not let us discern, in the diagram above, the fact that many stretches of the pre-modern world economic history were characterized by dynamics that was comparatively no less dramatic. For example, as soon as we "zoom in" on the apparently boringly flat stretch of the diagram above up to 800 BCE, we see the following completely dynamic picture (see Diagram 3.19):

Diagram 3.19. World GDP Growth from 25000 BCE up to 800 BCE
(in billions of 1990 PPP international dollars)

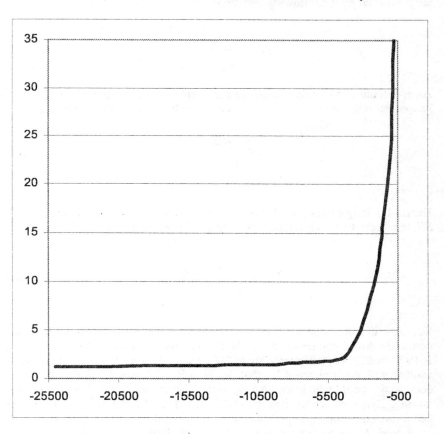

This, of course, is accounted for by the difference in scales. During the "iron revolution" the World System economic growth was extremely fast in comparison with all the earlier epochs; however, according to DeLong's estimates in absolute scale it constituted less than $10 billion a century. At present the world GDP increases by $10 billion at average every three days (World Bank 2005). As a result, even the period of relatively fast World System economic growth in the age of the "iron revolution" looks like an almost horizontal line in comparison with the stretch of the modern economic growth. In other words the impression of the pre-modern economic stagnation created by Diagram 3.18 could be regarded as an illusion (in the strictest sense of this word) produced just by the quadratic-hyperbolic trend of the world GDP growth up to 1973.

We have already mentioned that, as has been shown by von Foerster, von Hoerner and Kapitza the world population growth before the 1970s is very well approximated by the following equation:

$$N = \frac{C}{t_0 - t} . \tag{2.1}$$

As according to the model under consideration S can be approximated as kN, its long term dynamics can be approximated with the following equation:

$$S = \frac{kC}{t_0 - t} . \tag{3.13}$$

Hence, the long-term dynamics of the most dynamical part of the world GDP, SN, the world surplus product, can be approximated as follows:

$$SN = \frac{kC^2}{(t_0 - t)^2} . \tag{3.14}$$

Note that if von Foerster, Mora, and Amiot had had at their disposal, in addition to the world population data, also the data on the world GDP dynamics for 1–1973 (published, however, only in 2001 by Maddison) they could have made another striking "prediction" – that on Saturday, 23 July, 2005 an "economic doomsday" would take place; that is, on that day the world GDP would become infinite. They would have also found that in 1–1973 CE the world GDP growth had followed quadratic-hyperbolic rather than simple hyperbolic pattern.

Indeed, Maddison's estimates of the world GDP dynamics for 1–1973 CE are almost perfectly approximated by the following equation:

$$G = \frac{C}{(t_0 - t)^2} , \tag{3.15}$$

where G is the world GDP, $C = 17355487.3$ and $t_0 = 2005.56$ (see Diagram 3.20):

Diagram 3.20. World GDP dynamics, 1–1973 CE
(in billions of 1990 international dollars, PPP):
the fit between predictions of quadratic-hyperbolic
model and the observed data

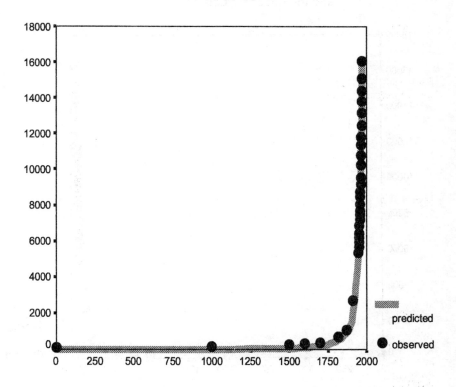

NOTE: $R = 0.9993$, $R^2 = 0.9986$, $p \ll 0.0001$. The black markers correspond to Maddison's (2001) estimates (Maddison's estimates of the world per capita GDP for 1000 CE has been corrected on the basis of Meliantsev [1996: 55–97]). The grey solid line has been generated by the following equation: $G = \dfrac{17749573.1}{(2006 - t)^2}$. The best-fit values of parameters C (17749573.1) and t_0 (2006) have been calculated with the least squares method (actually, as was mentioned above, the best fit is achieved with $C = 17355487.3$ and $t_0 = 2005.56$ [which gives just the "doomsday Saturday, 23 July, 2005"], but we have decided to keep hereafter to the integer year numbers).

In fact, the fit provided by the simple hyperbolic model for the world GDP dynamics for 1–1973 CE is also in no way bad, but still less perfect than the one found for the quadratic hyperbolic model (see Diagram 3.21):

Diagram 3.21. World GDP dynamics, 1–1973 CE
(in billions of 1990 international dollars, PPP):
the fit between predictions of hyperbolic model
and the observed data

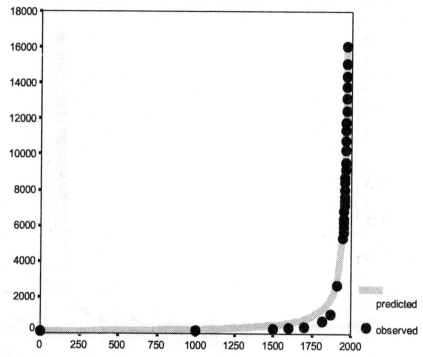

NOTE: $R = 0.9978$, $R^2 = 0.9956$, $p \ll 0.0001$. The black markers correspond to Maddison's (2001) estimates (Maddison's estimates of the world per capita GDP for 1000 CE has been corrected on the basis of Meliantsev [1996: 55–97]). The grey solid line has been generated by the following equation: $G = \dfrac{227906.1}{1987 - t}$. The best-fit values of parameters C (227906.1) and t_0 (1987) have been calculated with the least squares method.

This, of course, suggests that the long-term dynamics of the world GDP up to the 1970s should be approximated better with a quadratic rather than simple hyperbola.

Note that, on the other hand, the simple hyperbolic model does fit the world population dynamics in 1–1973 much better than the world GDP one. Indeed, though the world 1–1973 CE GDP dynamics fits the simple hyperbolic model of type (2.1) rather well ($R = 0.9978$, $R^2 = 0.9956$, $p \ll 0.0001$), this fit is still significantly worse than the one observed for the world population growth for the same time ($R = 0.9996$, $R^2 = 0.9991$, $p \ll 0.0001$) (see Diagram 3.22):

Diagram 3.22. World population dynamics, 1–1973 CE (in millions): the fit between predictions of hyperbolic model and the observed data

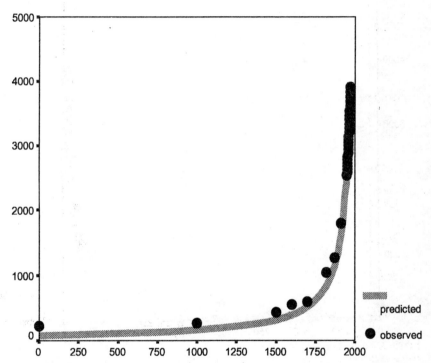

NOTE: $R = 0.9996$, $R^2 = 0.9991$, $p \ll 0.0001$. The black markers correspond to Maddison's (2001) estimates. The grey solid line has been generated by the following equation: $N = \dfrac{163158.78}{2014 - t}$. The best-fit values of parameters C (163158.78) and t_0 (2014) have been calculated with the least squares method.

However, the quadratic hyperbolic model renders a worse fit for the world population ($R = 0.9982$, $R^2 = 0.9963$, $p \ll 0.0001$) (see Diagram 3.23):

Diagram 3.23. World population dynamics, 1–1973 CE (in millions): the fit between predictions of quadratic-hyperbolic model and the observed data

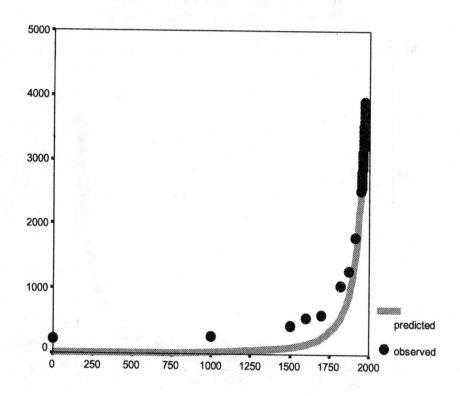

NOTE: $R = 0.9982$, $R^2 = 0.9963$, $p \ll 0.0001$. The black markers correspond to Maddison's (2001) estimates. The grey solid line has been generated by the following equation: $N = \dfrac{33505220.7}{(2065 - t)^2}$. The best-fit values of parameters C (33505220.702) and t_0 (2065) have been calculated with the least squares method.

Thus, up to the 1970s the hyperbolic growth of the world population was accompanied by the quadratic-hyperbolic growth of the world GDP, just as is suggested by our model.

Chapter 4

A General Extended Macromodel of World Economic, Cultural, and Demographic Growth

One problem with the compact macromodels is that they do not account for the post-1962 world population growth pattern. Take, for example, our simulation with the first macromodel starting in 1650, which produced an almost perfect fit with the observed data for 1650–1962. After 1962 (and especially after 1985) the gap between the predictions generated by the compact macromodel and observed values of the world population starts growing in a literally hyperbolic way (see Diagram 4.1):

Diagram 4.1.   Growth of the Gap between Predicted and Observed Values, 1985–2003

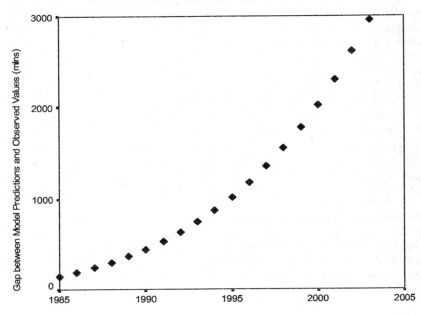

Our general extended macromodel of the world's economic, cultural, and demographic growth is conceived to capture both of its two salient features: [1] hyperbolic growth trend in the pre-1962 era, and [2] increasing decline of the world population growth rates afterwards.

Earlier researchers differ significantly in their analytical attempts to integrate into one model the model of hyperbolic growth and the model of global demographic transition. Kapitza (1992, 1999) connects the cause of the transition with the limited nature of the characteristic times of the human development and the humankind development.[1] Kremer (1993) considers the cause to be the decline of fertility in wealthy families. There are also differences in the levels of their approach: Kremer tries to describe the actual mechanism of transition, whereas Kapitza does not look for the actual mechanism of fertility reduction; he rather looks for the cause of the change of the regime in the global development of humankind. Kapitza tries to explain why the current state is exceptional, why the global demographic transition is taking place just now within a period of time that is microscopic on the historical scale, and just on the level of development that has been achieved at the moment.

In the model suggested by us below we aim at accounting both for the transition micromechanism and for the causes of the uniqueness of this phenomenon. The first thing which should be defined is the time period within which the respective model could claim to describe reality.

We have world population estimates starting from 1 million BP, and this is the period for which the population growth is analyzed by Kapitza and Kremer. Despite all the attractiveness of such global theories, we will consciously restrict the scale of our analysis. As in addition to population we use other indices (in particular the world GDP), the field of our model applicability is naturally restricted by the field of available statistical data. This does not mean that the model is not applicable to earlier times, but in any case to corroborate this one would need more data than is available at present.

More or less grounded estimates of the world GDP are available now for the period since 1 CE (Maddison 1995, 2001). Since 1950 they are known at a rather high level of accuracy for every year (Maddison 2001; World Bank 2005). Thus our model only describes demographic and techno-economic growth from 1 CE until the present. The prognostic potential of the model is also restricted by time of the order of one century, which will be discussed specially below.

The uniqueness of the current sharp decrease of the world population growth rates consists in the fact that for the first time in the world history it is connected with the global decline of fertility rates. All the previous decreases took place because of increases in the rate of mortality due to famines, epidemics, warfare *etc.* In the framework of the global demographic process just this

---

[1] For more detail see Appendix 3.

appears to constitute the uniqueness of the present time, for which Kapitza tried to account. Indeed, in comparison with all the previous development of humankind, it is precisely our time that marks the transition to a new demographic regime.

Thus, the model involving the global demographic transition should detect factors causing this transition, and first of all the factors of sharp fertility reduction.

Kremer attempted to account for fertility decline through the introduction of the function of dependence of fertility on income (Diagram 3.1). However such an explanation is not sufficient and rather indicates a mediated relationship. Thus, the drop in per capita incomes in the countries of the former Communist block in the late 1980s and 1990s did not lead to sharp rise of fertility rates, as one would expect from Kremer's model; in fact we observe the exact reverse (see, *e.g.*, Korotayev, Malkov, and Khaltourina 2005: 255–81). In addition to this, the introduction of additional nonlinear functions including several parameters, each of which is poorly measured in historical perspective, significantly decreases the possibility to use the model for the description of actual data.

To determine the main factors and predictors of fertility reduction it makes sense to address the empirical data. Analyses of large amounts of empirical data suggest that one of the major factors of fertility reduction (in addition to, *e.g.*, the development of health care, or social security subsystems) is the growth of education (especially, female education) (*e.g.*, Hollingsworth 1996; McMichael 2001; Bongaarts 2003 *etc.*).

The literacy rate (that is, the proportion of literate people in the adult population) turns out to be a good integral indicator of the education level. Note that it has been shown that female literacy turns out to be a rather strong negative predictor of fertility (*e.g.*, Bongaarts 2003).

Our own cross-national test of fertility factors with stepwise multiple regression has confirmed this conclusion (see Table 4.1):

Table 4.1.   Regression Model of Fertility Factors in the World in 1995

Model	Nonstadardized Coefficients		Standardized Coefficient	t	p
	B	Standard Error	β		
Constant	6.955	0.467		14.899	4×10^{-16}
Female Literacy, %	- 0.038	0.007	- 0.600	- 5.139	0.00001
Number of Physicians per 1000	- 0.253	0.117	- 0.239	- 2.155	0.036
Urbanization (% of population, leaving in cities)	- 0.006	0.007	- 0.087	- 0.866	0.391

NOTE: $R = 0.837$; $R^2 = 0.701$; $p = 2 \times 10^{-11}$. DATA SOURCE: SPSS 2005.

This three-factor model accounts for more than 70% of all the variation of fertility rates in 1995. This multiple regression analysis confirms that female literacy is a major factor in fertility reduction in the course of modernization (let us note here that – as we shall see below – female, male and overall literacy are very strongly interconnected variables).

Our regression analysis of the World Bank (2005) and US Bureau of the Census (2005) data on the female literacy and world population growth rates has produced the following results (see Tables 4.2 and 4.3):

Table 4.2. World Population and Female Literacy, 1990–1999

Year	World Population Growth Rate (%)	World Literacy Rate, adult female (% of females, ages 15 and above)
1990	1.58	61.61
1991	1.56	62.38
1992	1.49	63.13
1993	1.44	63.90
1994	1.43	64.66
1995	1.38	65.44
1996	1.37	66.56
1997	1.32	67.71
1998	1.29	68.60
1999	1.25	69.50

Table 4.3. Correlation between World Population Size and Female Literacy, 1990–1999 (regression analysis)

Model	Unstandardized Coefficients		Standardized Coefficients	t	Sig.
	B	Std. Error	Beta		
(Constant)	4.054	0.162		25.003	0.00000001
Literacy rate, adult female (% of females, ages 15 and above)	-0.04044	0.002	-0.985	-16.312	0.0000002

Dependent Variable: **World Population Annual Growth Rate** (%)

$R = 0.971$, $R^2 = 0.967$

As we see, we do observe an extremely strong and significant correlation in the predicted direction. In fact, this regression analysis suggests that 96.7% of all the world macrodemographic variation in 1990–1999 is described by the following equation:

$$r = 4.05 - 0.0404F,$$

where F is world female literacy (%), and r is the annual population growth rate (%).

Note that this model predicts that when the world population literacy becomes 100% (which by definition implies 100% female literacy), the world population growth rate will be 0.01% (4.05 − 0.0404 × 100), which is extremely close to the one of the main assumptions of our model below.

Thus, there are definite grounds to consider literacy as a good integral index of those modernization processes that could be considered as fertility reduction factors. The fertility decline in connection with the growing literacy rate is free from the defects of Kremer's explanation connecting the declining fertility directly with growing incomes. Our explanation has no problem with the above cited case of the decreasing incomes not being accompanied by increasing fertility in the post-Communist countries (in the late 1980s and early 1990s). On the other hand, the suggested explanation is wider than Kremer's in the sense that literate people tend to earn more than the illiterate ones. Thus, Kremer's explanation only works in the periods of stability, whereas our explanation works both for stable and crisis periods.

We would like to stress that in no way are we going to claim that the literacy growth is the only factor in the demographic transition. We do not deny important roles played by such factors as the development of medical care, or social security subsystems (*e.g.*, Chesnais 1992). Note that these variables together with literacy can be regarded as different parameters of one integrative variable – the human capital development index (*e.g.*, Denison 1962; Schultz 1963; Lucas 1988; Scholing and Timmermann 1988; Meliantsev 1996, 2003, 2004a, 2004b). On the other hand, both of these variables display a very strong correlation with literacy.[2] In general, if we know that in country A the proportion of literate population is 95%, and in country B this proportion is 25%, we can be perfectly sure that the health care and social security subsystems in country A are about an order of magnitude more developed than in country B. Note also that the modern medical care development is connected in the most direct way with the development of the education subsystem. The development and diffusion of new medical technologies (including, naturally, the family planning ones) is very strongly connected with the development of education.

---

[2] For example, our cross-national analysis of *World Development Indicators* database for the year 1975 shows that there is a strong and significant correlation between total literacy rate and the percentage of birth attended by skilled personnel ($R = 0.83$; $p < 0.0001$, similar results were obtained for other years) (World Bank 2005). On the other hand, our analysis of the data for the year 1995 indicates that literacy rate below 30% predicts with the maximum possible value (Gamma = 1.0) social security taxes being below 5% of current revenue, and literacy rate below 75% predicts in the same way security taxes being below 15% of current revenue. We have also found that the number of physicians per 1,000 correlates exponentially with the total literacy rate for the same year ($R = 0.844$) (In this case the data on literacy are from World95 database [SPSS 2005]; the data on other parameters are from *World Development Indicators* Database [World Bank 2005]).

E.g., the medical specialists are produced by the education system, the education facilitates the spread of medical information (including the information on family planning means and practices), and so on.

Thus, literacy rate turns out to be a very strong predictor of the development of both medical care and social security subsystems.

Hence, literacy has turned out to be a rather sensitive indicator of human capital development level, which has made it possible to avoid including its other parameters as separate variables in our model.

Note that the overall adult literacy turns out to be an extremely strong predictor of both male and female literacy (see Table 4.4):

Table 4.4.   Correlations between World Overall, Female, and Male Literacy Rates, 1970–1999

		Literacy rate, adult total (% of people ages 15 and above)	Literacy rate, adult female (% of females ages 15 and above)	Literacy rate, adult male (% of males ages 15 and above)
Literacy rate, adult total (% of people ages 15 and above)	Pearson Correlation		0.99984	0.99977
	Sig. (2-tailed)		<<0.0001	<<0.0001
	N		30	30
Literacy rate, adult female (% of females ages 15 and above)	Pearson Correlation	0.99984		0.99923
	Sig. (2-tailed)	<<0.0001		<<0.0001
	N	30		30
Literacy rate, adult male (% of males ages 15 and above)	Pearson Correlation	0.99977	0.99923	
	Sig. (2-tailed)	<<0.0001	<<0.0001	
	N	30	30	

Correlations of such a level could, of course, hardly be regarded as anything but extremely strong, even notwithstanding the fact that here we are dealing with an evident autocorrelation component. That is why, though the effects of male and female literacy on demographic dynamics are rather different, it has turned out to be possible to avoid including them as separate variables in model.

An important additional factor that led us to choose literacy rather than any other fertility reducing parameter of the human capital development index is that this seems to be the only such parameter for which it appears possible to obtain long-term global historical data.

As a result, in order to account for the global demographic transition, model (3.7)-(3.10) should be extended to take into account the development of human capital level (measured through literacy rate) as a factor of fertility decrease. As a result of this modification, model (3.7)-(3.10) looks as follows:

$$\frac{dN}{dt} = aNS\ (1 - L)\ , \tag{4.1}$$

$$\frac{dS}{dt} = bNS\ , \tag{3.10}$$

$$\frac{dL}{dt} = cLS\ (1 - L)\ , \tag{4.2}$$

where L is proportion of literate population and a, b, and c are constants. The influence of world literacy on the global demographic transition is expressed through the addition to (3.7) of the multiplier $(1 - L)$, which results in equation (4.1). Such a modification implies that the growth of literacy affects negatively fertility rates even in the absence of any resource limitations. As regards the fact that the death rates also decline with modernization, equation (4.1) takes this fact into account too, since the natural population growth rate (which tends to zero when the literacy approaches to 100%) is, by definition, the difference between the fertility rate and the death rate.

The introduced additional equation for the literacy growth (4.2) has the following sense: the literacy growth rate is proportional to the proportion of literate people in the whole population L (potential teachers), to the proportion of illiterate people in the whole population $(1 - L)$ (potential pupils), and the presence of surplus S, which can be used for educational purposes (in addition to this, S is connected with the technological level T, including the level of educational technologies that accelerate the spread of education). From the mathematical point of view equation (4.2) is analogous to logistic equation (0.2), because within equation (4.2) the saturation is achieved with literacy level $L = 1$, whereas S accounts for the speed with which the saturation level is reached.

Notwithstanding the fact that this modification of the model is generally quite logical, its version (4.1) – (3.10) – (4.2) needs additional justification. As it is evident that with the same logical conclusions on the dependence of population growth rate on the literacy rate (or, on the dependence of literacy growth rate on the growth rate of the number of potential teachers *etc.*) the same model may be presented as:

$$\frac{dN}{dt} = aN^{\varphi_1} S^{\varphi_2} (1 - L)^{\varphi_3}\ ,$$

$$\frac{dS}{dt} = bN^{\varphi_4} S^{\varphi_5}\ ,$$

$$\frac{dL}{dt} = cL^{\varphi_6} S^{\varphi_7} (1 - L)^{\varphi_8}\ ,$$

where φ_1, φ_2, φ_3, φ_4, φ_5, φ_6, φ_7, φ_8 are some positive values that are not necessarily equal to one.

As regards coefficients φ_1, φ_2, φ_4, φ_5, the following suggests that they could be considered to be equal to one: in the area, which is removed from the zone of the second phase of the global demographic transition, such coefficients describe satisfactorily the hyperbolic growth and fit the empirical data very well (see Chapter 3). As regards values of the other coefficients, they should be also determined on the basis of empirical data.

It is easy to notice that if $\varphi_1 = \varphi_6 = 1$, $\varphi_2 = \varphi_7$, $\varphi_3 = \varphi_8$, through the dividing of the first equation by the third we arrive at the following equation:

$$\frac{dN}{dL} = \frac{a}{c}\frac{N}{L}.$$

Its solution defines the relationship between L and N in the following way:

$$L = \lambda N^{\frac{c}{a}}, \qquad (4.3)$$

where λ is a constant.

Let us test this hypothesis with historical data. Diagram 4.2 presents data on the simultaneous growth of world literacy and world population in double logarithmic scale:

Diagram 4.2. World Literacy (%) and World Population (millions)

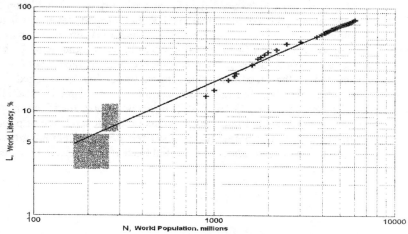

NOTE: Rectangles correspond to 1 and 1000 CE, for which we have large dispersions of estimates. Estimates of the world population are by Kremer (1993), Maddison (2001) and US Bureau of the Census (2005). World literacy = proportion of literate adult population, calculated on the basis of Meliantsev's (1996, 2003, 2004a, 2004b) estimates and UNESCO/World Bank (2005) data for post-1970 period.

Within such a scale a straight line corresponds to a power-law dependence. The diagram suggests that power-law dependence (4.3) fits the available data rather well.

Thus, the available data (see Diagram 4.2) suggest the validity of relation (4.3), and thus argue in favor of the statement that $\varphi_1 = \varphi_6 = 1$, $\varphi_2 = \varphi_7$, $\varphi_3 = \varphi_8$, which, in view of our earlier estimate of the power of φ_2 as 1.0, may be written as: $\varphi_1 = \varphi_6 = \varphi_2 = \varphi_7 = 1$, $\varphi_3 = \varphi_8$. As regards the equality of φ_3 to 1.0, what supports this is the good fit (see Diagrams 4.3–8) of the observed data with the values generated by model (4.1)-(3.10)-(4.2). Of course, a finer "tuning" of the model using parameters $\varphi_{1...8}$ could enhance the fit, however, due to the high error margins for existing data such a "fine tuning" does not make much sense, as we do not know for sure the exact coordinates of the points to which the solution should be tuned. In any case, within such a general model one should strive to decrease the number of those parameters that do not enhance the solution at a qualitative level.

The results of computer simulation with (4.1)-(3.10)-(4.2) with parameters

$a = 1.085 \cdot 10^{-5}$ ($\$ \cdot$ year)$^{-1}$;
$b = 6.51 \cdot 10^{-12}$ (person $\cdot$ year)$^{-1}$;
$c = 8.2 \cdot 10^{-6}$ ($\$ \cdot$ year)$^{-1}$;
$\tilde{m}$ ("necessary product per person") = 420 \$

and initial conditions for 1 CE:

$N_0 = 170000000$;
$S_0 = 17.47$ \$;
$L_0 = 0.052$,

where L is a dimensionless quantity (ranging from 0 to 1), sign \$ corresponds to 1995 international dollar (PPP), are displayed at Diagrams 4.3–8:

Diagram 4.3. World Population Growth

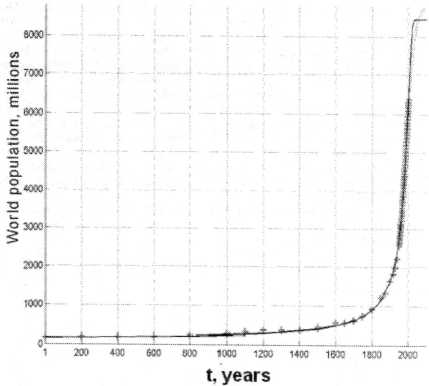

t, years

Values generated by the model (solid line) for the world population describe well both the pre-1962 hyperbolic growth and the global demographic transition by the present (the observed values are indicated with grey crosses). With regards to the future, the model suggests a scenario a bit different from the intermediate UN forecast (light grey markers). The model suggests that at the final phases the global demographic tradition will proceed in a less smooth way than is implied by the UN forecasts.

A smoother transition could be achieved through the introduction of $\varphi_3 = \varphi_8 \neq 1$; however, the UN forecast is just one of many possible forecasts that rely on their own models. On the other hand, the available historical data are not sufficiently exact to support the hypothesis $\varphi_3 = \varphi_8 \neq 1$.

Naturally, with appearance of new data the model could be corrected.

Diagram 4.4. World GDP Growth

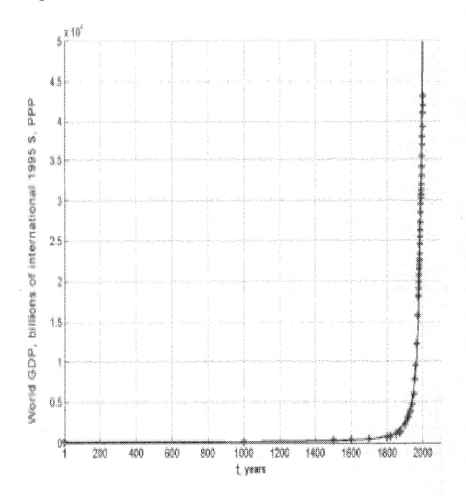

The world GDP grew even more steeply than the world population and can be described mathematically with equation (3.11). Notwithstanding the fact that GDP is not included explicitly in the system of equations, in this diagram the respective points are calculated on the basis of equations (3.10) and (4.1).

Finally, consider the diagram displaying the relationship between the world literacy growth dynamics generated by the model and the observed values of the respective variable (see Diagram 4.5):

Diagram 4.5.   World Literacy Growth (%%)

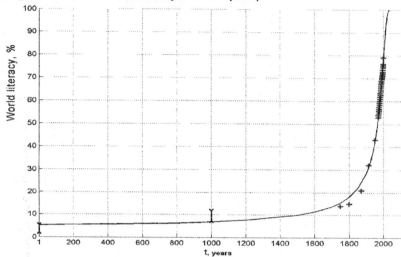

Diagrams in double logarithmic scale hide the visual component of hyperbolic growth and make the results more visible, though the deviations also look more saliently in this scale (Diagrams 4.6–8):

Diagram 4.6.   World Population Growth in Double Logarithmic Scale

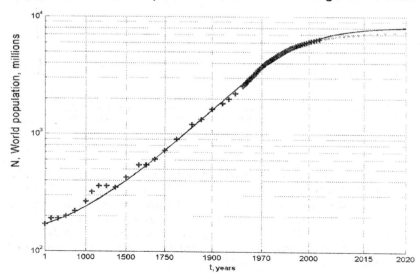

Diagram 4.7.   World GDP Growth in Double Logarithmic Scale

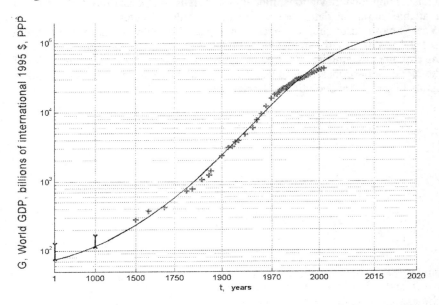

Diagram 4.8.   World Literacy Growth in Double Logarithmic Scale

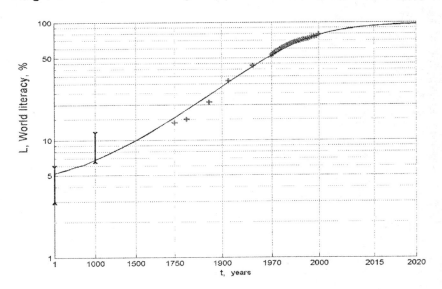

While commenting on these diagrams, it appears necessary to note that, not-withstanding local deviations, model (4.1)-(3.10)-(4.2) describes quite well the available empirical data, though the model only includes three coefficients. What is more, through normalization it appears possible to reduce two of them to 1.0 – in this case the model will only include one coefficient that is equal to the exponent in equation (4.3). Thus, notwithstanding the extreme simplicity of the model, it describes very successfully the joint dynamics of three major indicators of the global evolution of humankind.

Chapter 5

A Special Extended Macromodel of World Economic, Cultural, and Demographic Growth

In this model we make the following additional assumptions: (1) a literate population makes more technological innovations than an illiterate one. Consequently, literacy growth leads to acceleration of technological development. (2) In the Modern era the level of the World System's economic development is determined first of all by the level of development of human capital, which, we believe, can be roughly estimated by the world literacy level. These assumptions in conjunction with the assumptions of the models presented above suggest the following functional scheme of relationships between modeled subsystems (see Diagram 5.1):

Diagram 5.1. Functional Scheme of Relationships between Model Subsystems

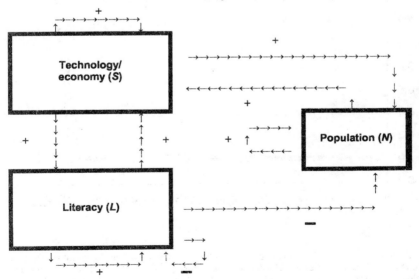

The relationships between these three subsystems are modeled using the following set of differential equations:

$$\frac{dN}{dt} = aSN(1 - L),$$

$$\frac{dS}{dt} = bLN,$$

$$\frac{dL}{dt} = cSL(1 - L),$$

where L is the proportion of the literate population and a, b, and c are constants.

This model generates dynamics shown in Diagram 5.2:

Diagram 5.2.   Dynamics Generated by the Model

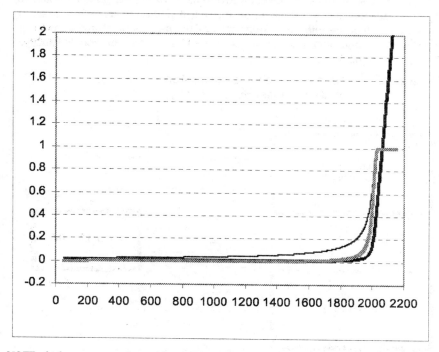

NOTE: *thick grey curve* – the world population counted as proportion from its size at stabilization level; *thin black curve* – literacy; *thick black curve* – level of the World System techno-economic development (S) counted as proportion from its level at world population stabilization point.

With such a compact model we are able to reproduce rather well both the hyperbolic growth of world population before 1962/3, and the subsequent increasing slow down of world population growth rates.

With our three-equation model we start the simulation in 1875 and do annual iterations with difference equations derived from the differential ones. We choose the following values of the constants and initial conditions: N = 1325 million; K = 1; L = 0.22[1]; a = 0.008 (this corresponds to the initial annual population growth rate and equals the average annual population growth rate in 1875–1900 CE according to Kremer's estimations [1993]); b = 0.00005; c = 0.007. The outcome of the simulation, presented in Diagram 5.3 indicates that irrespective of all its simplicity the model is actually capable of replicating quite reasonably the population estimates of Kremer (1993), US Bureau of the Census (2005) and other sources (Thomlinson 1975; Durand 1977; McEvedy and Jones 1978: 342–51; Biraben 1980; Haub 1995: 5; UN Population Division 2005; World Bank 2005) in most of their characteristics and in terms of the important turning points:

Diagram 5.3. Predicted and Observed Dynamics of World Population Growth, in millions

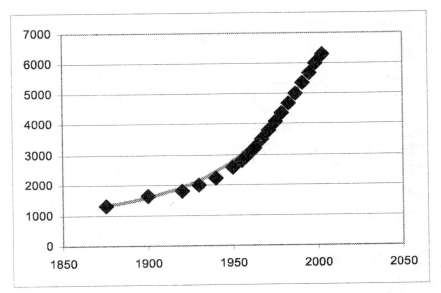

NOTE: The solid grey curve has been generated by the model; black markers correspond to the estimates of world population by Kremer (1993) for pre-1950 period, and the US Bureau of Census world population data for 1950–2003.

---

[1] Based on Meliantsev's (1996, 2003, 2004a, 2004b) estimates.

The correlation between the predicted and observed values for this simulation looks as follows: $R = 0.9989$, $R^2 = 0.9978$, $p \ll 0.0001$ (Diagram 5.4):

Diagram 5.4. World Population: Correlation between Predicted and Observed Values

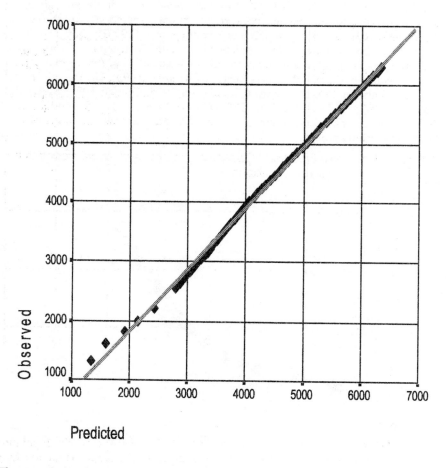

The correlation between predicted and observed values of world literacy also turns out to be rather high (see Diagram 5.5):

Diagram 5.5.   World Literacy, Proportion of Literate Adult Population:
Correlation between Predicted and Observed Values

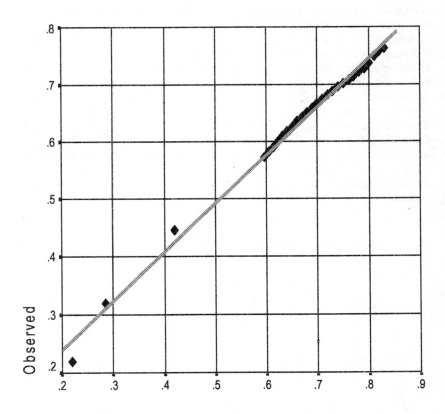

World Literacy, Proportion of Literate Adult Population: Predicted

$R = 0.997$, $R^2 = 0.994$, p << 0.0001

This dynamics has exact parallels in the real world – the world population
growth rates increased most rapidly when the world literacy was approaching
50% (as both in the model and in reality, the stretch between 30% and 70%
was passed within just a few decades compared with millennia during which
the first 10% were passed), they achieved their highest levels when the world
literacy rate was around 50%, and started decreasing with a progressively am-

plifying speed almost immediately after it grew over 50% (cp. Kremer 1993: 683; US Census Bureau 2005; World Bank 2005).[2]

Of course, the special macromodel has a much narrower applicability than the general ones. For example, it does not work at all for the preliterate period of human history, as, according to the special macromodel, zero literacy would correspond to a zero rate of techno-economic and demographic growth, whereas this does not match the reality at all. On the other hand, the special macromodel describe rather well the modernization period, which appears to reflect the fact that the development of human capital became the most important factor of economic development (see, e.g.: Meliantsev 1996; Dobrynin, Dyatlov, and Kurganskij 1999; Denison 1962; Schultz 1963; Scholing and Timmermann 1988; Lucas 1988 etc.). Note that, as we shall see below (see Chapter 7), the literacy level could serve as a rather sensitive indicator of the overall level of human capital development. Note also that we have at our disposal some data suggesting that the growth of literacy could serve in itself as a powerful factor of economic development; this will be discussed in the next chapter.

---

[2] Thus, it turns out that the sets of 2–3 differential equations specified above account for up to 99.78 per cent of all the variation in demographic, economic, and cultural macrodynamics of the world in the last 2,000–25,000 years. In fact, in some sense the second part of our *Introduction to Social Macrodynamics* (*Secular Cycles and Millennial Trends*) will be concerned with the remaining 0.22–0.34% (As was indicated above, the simulation with compact macromodel 1 started in 500 BCE [and run till 1962 CE] already gave a correlation with observed data as high as 0.9983 [$R^2 = 0.9966$], whereas in the second part of our *Introduction* we will be dealing mainly with the last two millennia of the world history). As we will see, to account for the remaining fraction of the variation is much more difficult, and we will only be able to start this process. What is more, the models will become more and more bulky, less and less elegant. However, in many senses this remaining fraction of variation is much more interesting than 99.66–99.78% of it, as without accounting for it we shall never be able to make any specific, concrete and exact predictions.

Chapter 6

Reconsidering Weber:
Literacy and the Spirit of Capitalism

In his classic *The Protestant Ethic and the Spirit of Capitalism*, Max Weber suggested that Protestantism stimulated the development of modern capitalism in Europe and North America. Weber disregarded the wide-spread explanation of economic success of Protestants in Europe in the Modern Age as a result of their religious minority position. He pointed out that Germen Catholics did not achieve the same results despite being a religious minority in many parts of Germany.

Weber explained significant differences between Catholics and Protestants in their social status and economic success through the different world views inherent in the doctrines of these two confessions. He suggested that a decisive role was played by the formation of a special "spirit of capitalism", which included the devotion to one's business, the desire to increase one's wealth in an honest way and so on. According to Weber, the spiritual basis of capitalism was grounded in the vulgarized versions of the theology of Calvinism and some other Protestant sects. It was, above all, the belief in predestination and (in vulgarized versions) in the possibility of obtaining the signs of whether one is predestined to salvation, via perfection in one's profession.

Many of Weber's followers tended to exaggerate the effect of religious ethics on the economic dynamics. Yet, Weber himself wrote:

"... however, we have no intention whatever of maintaining such a foolish and doctrinaire thesis as that the spirit of capitalism... could have only arisen as the result of certain effect of the Reformation, or even that capitalism as an economic system is a creation of the Reformation." (Weber 1972: 109).

Yet, this doctrinaire thesis is still frequently attributed to Weber (see, *e.g.*, Maddison 2001: 45). At the same time Weber, to our opinion, showed quite convincingly that the processes of religious evolution can produce some independent effect on socioeconomic development. On the other hand, the special extended macromodel considered above suggests another explanation for the correlation between the spread of Protestantism and some increase in economic development, which has been noted by Weber.

As has been mentioned earlier, human capital development has been suggested as one of the most important factors of economic growth, whereas edu-

cation is considered to be one of the most important components of human
capital (see, *e.g.*, Schultz 1963, Denison 1962, Lucas 1988, Scholing and
Timmermann 1988 *etc.*). We tested our special macromodel in Chapter 5, and
one of the assumptions of this model was a significant positive effect of literacy level on economic growth. The model based on this condition corre-
sponded well with the historical data on the demographic, economic, and educational dynamics of the World System. Consequently, this hypothesis has
passed preliminary testing. Let us test it again using cross-national data.

In the 20th century mass literacy spread around the globe, and nowadays
differences in literacy levels between different countries tend to disappear. At
the same time, according to our hypothesis, the differences in economic developments of various countries are rooted in the period of the beginning of modernization era. Therefore, it seems reasonable to explore the connection between such indicators as GDP per capita at present and the literacy level in the
early 19th century.[1] For the data on these variables, as well as on GDP per capita in the early 19th century, see Table 6.1:

Table 6.1. GDP per capita in the Countries and Regions of the World
in 1800 (international $ 1980, PPP[2]), GDP per capita in 2000
(international $ 1995, PPP) and % of literate population in 1800

Country/region	GDP per capita in 2000 (interna-tional $ 1995, PPP)	GDP per capita in 1800 (interna-tional $ 1980, PPP)	% of literate population in 1800
USA	31338.3	690	58
Great Britain	22652.5	1030	55
Germany	23912.6	790	55
France	23225.2	750	38
Israel	18894.5		(35)
Japan	23828.1	420	33
Italy	22874.8	670	30
China	3547.4	500	20
Mexico	8182.2	690	11
Brazil	6780.7	580	8
Russia	6643.6	488	8
India	2229.3	440	5
Indonesia	2807.3	425	5
Egypt	3253.4	325	3
Sub-Saharan Africa	1557.3		(1)

---

[1] Since the indicators of educational level are strongly correlated with each other, the percentage of
literate population seems to be a good integral indicator of the level of education for the early
modernization period.
[2] Purchasing power parity

NOTE: The source of the data on GDP per capita and literacy rate in 1800 is Meliantsev 1996; on GDP per capita and the literacy rate in Russia in 1800 see Meliantsev 2003; on GDP per capita in the countries and regions of the world in 2000 see World Bank 2005. Our estimates are in parentheses.

The data in Table 6.1 show that the level of economic wealth in the early 19th century in various regions did not differ greatly enough to be considered the leading factor of economic differentiation between the regions later on. Thus, per capita GDP in Mexico was approximately equal to that in the USA. However, the literacy rates differed significantly.

The correlation between literacy rates in 1800 and per capita GDP in 2000 is presented in Diagram 6.1:

Diagram 6.1.   Scatterplot of Literacy Rates in 1800
(% of literate people among the adult population)
and per capita GDP Levels in 2000
(international $ 1995, PPP)

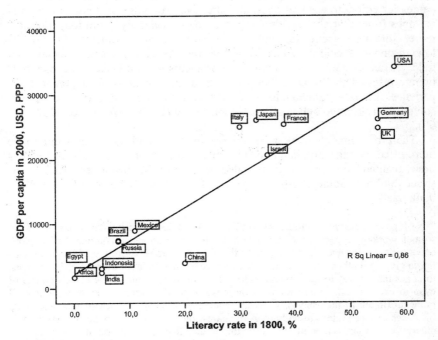

NOTE: $R = 0.93$; $R^2 = 0.86$; $p = 0.0000003$ (one-tailed).

Diagram 6.1 shows that there is a strong and definitely significant linear correlation between the literacy rate in 1800 and GDP per capita at present. R^2 coefficient indicates that this correlation explains 86% of the entire data dispersion.

Therefore, the hypothesis that the spread of literacy was one of the major factors of modern economic growth gains additional support. On the one hand, literate populations have many more opportunities to obtain and utilize the achievements of modernization than illiterate ones. On the other hand, literate people could be characterized by a greater innovative-activity level, which provides opportunities for modernization, development, and economic growth.

Literacy does not simply facilitate the process of perceiving innovation by an individual. It also changes her or his cognition to a certain extent. This problem was studied by Luria, Vygotsky, and Shemiakin, the famous Soviet psychologists, on the basis of the results of their fieldwork in Central Asia in the 1930s. Their study shows that education has a fundamental effect on the formation of cognitive processes (perception, memory, cognition). The researchers found out that illiterate respondents, unlike literate ones, preferred concrete names for colors to abstract ones, and situative groupings of items to categorical ones (note that abstract thinking is based on category cognition). Furthermore, illiterate respondents could not solve syllogistic problems like the following one – "Precious metals do not get rust. Gold is a precious metal. Can gold get rust or not?". These syllogistic problems did not make any sense to illiterate respondents because they were out of the sphere of their practical experience. Literate respondents who had at least minimal formal education solved the suggested syllogistic problems easily (Luria 1974, 1976, 1982: 47–69).

Therefore, literate workers, soldiers, inventors and so on turn out to be more effective than illiterate ones not only due to their ability to read instructions, manuals, and textbooks, but also because of the developed skills of abstract thinking. Some additional support for this could be found in Weber's book itself:

"The type of backward traditional form of labor is today very often exemplified by women workers, especially unmarried ones. An almost universal complaint of employers of girls, for instance German girls, is that they are almost entirely unable and unwilling to give up methods of work inherited or once learned in favor of more efficient ones, to adapt themselves to new methods, to learn and to concentrate their intelligence, or even to use it at all. Explanations of the possibility of making work easier, above all more profitable to themselves, generally encounter a complete lack of understanding. Increases of piece rates are without avail against the stone wall of habit. In general it is otherwise, and that is a point of no little importance from our view-point, only with girls having a specifically religious, especially a Pietistic, background" (Weber 1972: 75–6).

We believe that the above mentioned features of the behavior of German female workers in the late 19th–early 20th centuries simply reflects a relatively low educational level of German women from labor circles at that time. The spread of female literacy in Germany, as elsewhere, lagged behind that of male literacy (see Chapter 7). In the early 20th century the majority of women could write and read only in the most developed parts of Germany (Meliantsev 1996). More rational behavior of German workers from Pietistic circles could be easily explained by the special role of education in the lives of Protestants.

The ability to read was essential for Protestants (unlike Catholics) to perform their religious duty – to read the Bible. The reading of Holy Scripture was not just unnecessary for Catholic laymen, for a long time it was even prohibited for them. The edict of the Toulouse Synod (1229) prohibited the Catholic laymen from possessing copies of the Bible. Soon after that, a decision by the Tarragon Synod spread this prohibition to ecclesiastic people as well. In 1408, the Oxford Synod absolutely prohibited translations of the Holy Scripture. From the very beginning, Protestant groups did not accept this prohibition. Thus, Luther translated in 1522–1534 first the New Testament, and then the Old Testament, into German, so that any German-speaking person could read the Holy Scripture in his or her native language. Moreover, the Protestants viewed reading the Holy Scripture as a religious duty of any Christian. As a result, the level of literacy and education was, in general, higher for Protestants not only than it was for Catholics and for followers of other confessions that did not provide religious stimuli for learning literacy (see, for example: Malherbe 1997: 139–57).

In our opinion, this could explain to a considerable extent the differences between economic performance of the Protestants and the Catholics in the late 19th – early 20th centuries in Europe noticed by Weber. One of Weber's research goals was to show that religion can have independent influence on economic processes. The results of our study support this point. Indeed, spiritual leaders of Protestantism persuaded their followers to read the Bible not to support the economic growth but for religious reasons, which were formulated as a result of ideological processes that were rather independent of economic life. We do not question that specific features of Protestant ethics could have facilitated economic development. However, we believe that we found another (and probably more powerful) channel of Protestantism's influence on the economic growth of the Western countries.

Chapter 7

Extended Macromodels
and Demographic Transition Mechanisms

To start with, the compact macromodels we discussed specify only the most general mechanisms of world population growth. However, we also need to know how the macrotrends are produced on a more specific level. The population growth rate is a resultant of two determinant variables: fertility rate and mortality rate.[1] What kind of dynamics of these two variables could produce the observed demographic macrotrends?

The most evident more specific mechanism accounting for both the hyperbolic population growth in 1850–1962/3 and the "inverse hyperbolic" trend afterwards is the demographic transition itself (e.g., Chesnais 1992; Kapitza 1999). As is well known, during the first phase of demographic transition a rather sharp decline of mortality rates is observed. This is followed by decline in fertility rates (through the introduction of family planning practices and technologies as a proximate cause), but with a substantial time lag. As a result, for considerable periods of time we observe pronounced trends towards the rise of the population growth rates against the background of growing population. This, of course, produces just a hyperbolic effect – the higher is the population (N), the higher is the population growth rate (r). Since the 19th century more and more populations of the world entered the demographic transition. Till the 1960s the number of populations which entered the 2nd phase of the demographic transition did not compensate for the hyperbolic growth of the 1st phase populations; hence, the hyperbolic growth trend was characteristic not only for individual populations, but also for world population as a whole.

In fact, the demographic transition mechanism fits the compact macromodel rather well, specifying more concrete links between the variables in question. When the technology starts growing significantly faster than the population (in our simulation this process started in the 19th century and greatly accelerated in the 20th century, which correlates well with the observed data), this results in a significant growth of GDP per capita, and hence, per capita consumption,

---

[1] Of course, if we deal with population dynamics of individual countries we have also to take into account emigration and immigration rates. However, as the two respective variables do not affect the growth rate of the world population as a whole, we do not have to consider them on our level of analysis.

health status, and hence the decrease of mortality rates. With further growth of per capita GDP we have more and more investment in spheres other than the subsistence economy, including education. On the one hand, the growth of education further speeds up GDP growth through stimulating the increase of innovation rate, but on the other hand, it decreases fertility. In the compact macromodel this time lag is simulated in the following way: until literacy level reaches 50% the effect of the increase of this parameter on the growth of S (and consequently N) is felt much more strongly than the inverse effect of L on N, which results in hyperbolic population growth. This has evident correlates in the real world: growth of a literate minority, say, from 5 to 30% (against the background of rapidly growing overall population) would mean a tremendous increase of a number of potential effective innovators; what is more, due to the "nonrivalry of technology" effect discussed above, the innovations made by a literate minority can be used (and are used) by illiterate populations and for the benefit of illiterate populations. In the meantime the negative influence of female literacy on birth-rates (and, hence, the population growth rates) is still quite weak and does not counterweight the negative influence of the growing GDP per capita on mortality. Note that the growth of world literacy in this range did correlate with the increase in the population growth rates (see Diagram 7.1):

Diagram 7.1. World Population Literacy and World Population Growth Rates, 1000–1950

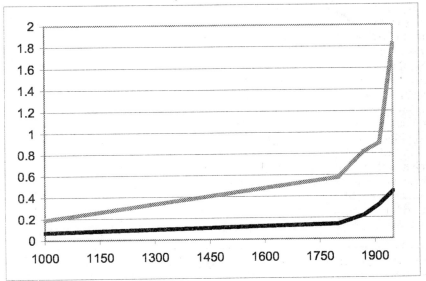

NOTES: *grey curve* – world population growth rates, % (Kremer 1993); *black curve* – world literacy, proportion of literate adult population, calculated on the basis of Meliantsev's (1996, 2003, 2004a, 2004b) estimates. $R = 0.961$, $R^2 = 0.924$, $p < 0.01$

As we shall see below, a similar relationship can be detected by cross-national comparisons for later periods. In the real world the mechanism specified above is further amplified by the fact that the growth of female literacy (which has the strongest negative effect on fertility rates, and hence on population growth rates) lags significantly behind male literacy. This lag is still visible even for the 1970–1999 period (see Diagram 7.2):

Diagram 7.2.   World Male and Female Literacy, 1970–1999 (World Bank 2005)

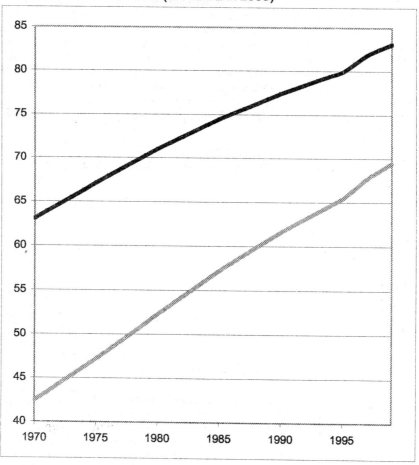

NOTES: *grey curve* – literacy rate, adult female (% of females ages 15 and above); *black curve* – literacy rate, adult male (% of males ages 15 and above).

In fact during this period, the growth of world literacy was accompanied by a decrease in the gap between the male and female literacy (see Diagram 7.3):

Diagram 7.3. World Overall Literacy and the Gap between Male and Female Literacy, 1970–1999 (World Bank 2005)

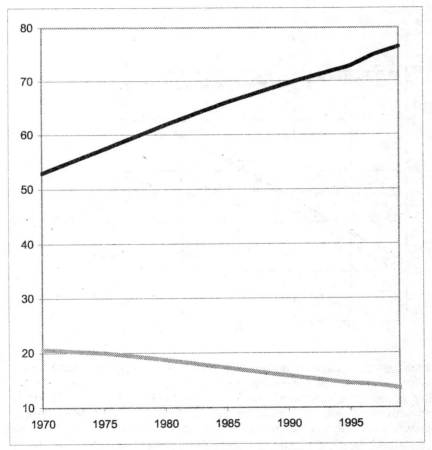

NOTES: *Black curve* – literacy rate, adult total (% of people ages 15 and above); *grey curve* – gap between male literacy rate, adult female (% of females ages 15 and above).

However, in the 5–30% range the gap between male and female literacy tended to grow (*e.g.*, Meliantsev 1996, 2003, 2004a, 2004b). Note that this pattern can also be detected through world-wide cross-national comparisons (see Diagram 7.4):

Diagram 7.4. Relationships between Overall Literacy (%, X-axis),
Female Literacy (%, Y-axis), Male Literacy (%, Y-axis),
Death Rates (‰, Y-axis), Birth Rates (‰, Y-axis),
and Population Growth Rates^2 (‰, Y-axis), nations
with overall adult literacy ≤ 30%, 1970 (World Bank
2005), scatterplot with fitted Lowess lines

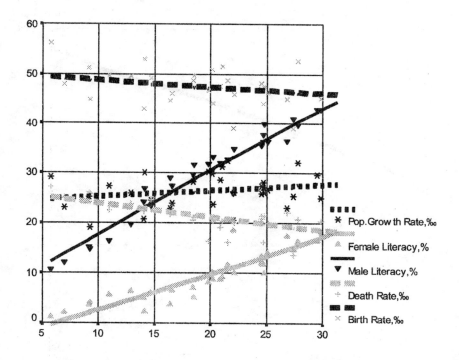

As we see, this suggests that even after 1962/3, in the range of 5–30% overall
literacy, female literacy tended to grow much slower than the male literacy.
Thus, in this range, economic growth (to a considerable extent supported by the
growth of overall literacy [e.g., Meliantsev 1996, 2003, 2004a, 2004b]) leads to
a rather rapid decline of mortality rates; however, the growth of female literacy
in this range tends to be too slow to produce as strong a negative effect on the

---

^{2} Internal ("natural") population growth rate calculated as birth rate minus death rate. We used this
variable instead of standard growth rate, as the latter takes into account the influence of emigration and immigration processes, which notwithstanding all their importance are not relevant for
the subject of this chapter, because though they could affect in a most significant way the population growth rates of particular countries, they do not affect the world population growth.

fertility rates. As a result, the growth of literacy in this range is usually accompanied by increase in population growth rates.

World Bank (2005) data suggest that world population growth rates started declining systematically after overall world literacy reached *c.* 50% (by which time the male literacy had increased up to *c.* 60%, and female literacy to *c.* 40%). Thus, after L increases over 50% its inversed effect on N growth rate becomes much stronger than the positive effect through S (which corresponds to the second phase of demographic transition). Note that a similar pattern can also be observed in individual demographic histories of particular countries (see, *e.g.*, Diagrams 7.5–6 below):

Diagram 7.5. Demographic and Literacy Dynamics in Ghana, 1970–1997 (World Bank 2005)

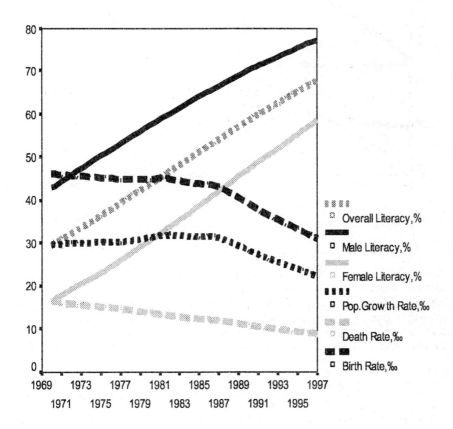

Diagram 7.6.   Demographic and Literacy Dynamics in Iran,
1970–2000 (World Bank 2005)

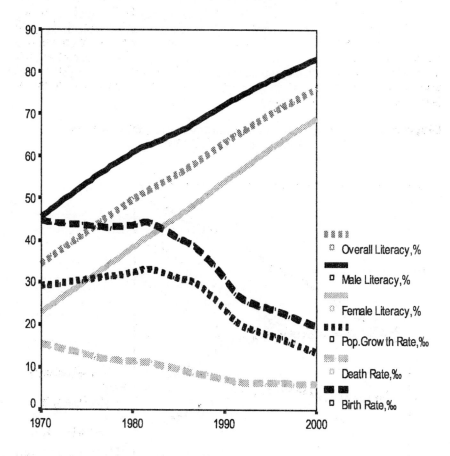

The inverse influence of above-50% literacy on population growth also can be easily detected through a world-wide cross-national comparison (see Diagram 7.7):

Diagram 7.7. Relationships between Overall Literacy (%, X-axis), Female Literacy (%, Y-axis), Male Literacy (%, Y-axis), Death Rates (‰, Y-axis), Birth Rates (‰, Y-axis), and Population Growth Rates (‰, Y-axis), nations with overall adult literacy 50–90%, 1970 (World Bank 2005), scatterplot with fitted Lowess lines

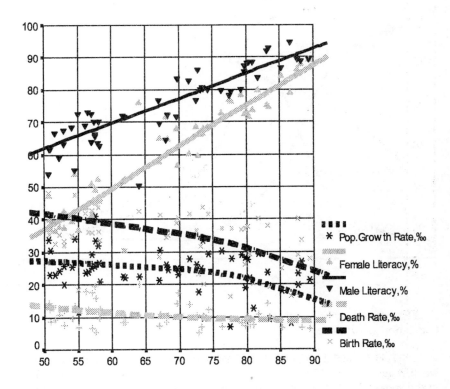

The demographic transition mechanism is usually illustrated with the following diagram (see Diagram 7.8):

Diagram 7.8.   Demographic Transition Dynamics
(from Kapitza 1999)

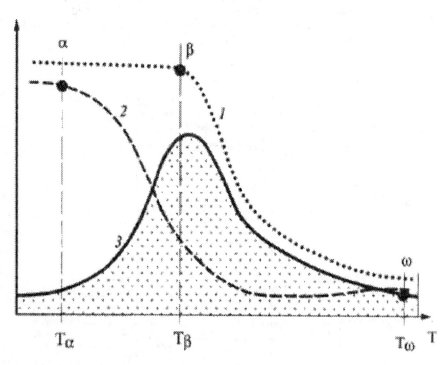

NOTES: *dotted curve* – birth rate; *punctuated curve* – death rate; *solid curve* – population growth rate.

Note that if we make a scatterplot of the type used above for the whole range, we will get death and birth rate curves that are quite similar to the ones found in the standard diagrams of demographic transition (except perhaps for its extreme left part, due to the fact that in world-wide databases for the late 20th century we hardly have any populations remaining in the very beginning of the demographic transition process) (see Diagram 7.9):

Diagram 7.9.   Relationships between Overall Literacy (%, X-axis),
Death Rates (‰, Y-axis), Birth Rates (‰, Y-axis),
1975 (World Bank 2005), scatterplot
with fitted Lowess lines

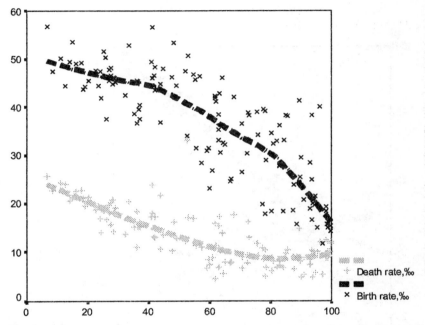

If we also plot curves for male and female literacy, we will see that they display an almost perfect mirror image of demographic transition curves (see Diagram 7.10):

Diagram 7.11. Relationships between Overall Literacy (%, X-axis),
Female Literacy (%, Y-axis), Male Literacy (%, Y-axis),
Death Rates (‰, Y-axis), and Birth Rates (‰, Y-axis),
1975 (World Bank 2005),
scatterplot with fitted Lowess lines

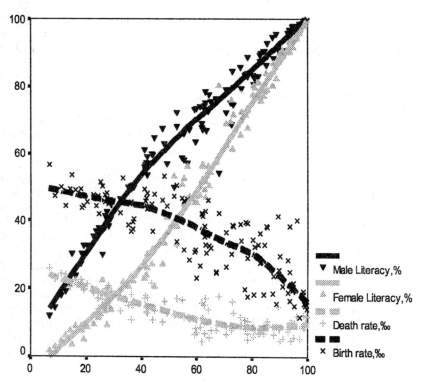

As we see in the left part of the diagram, the growing gap between male and female literacy is accompanied by the increasing gap between fertility and mortality (and, hence, increasing population growth rates), whereas in the right part of the diagram the decreasing gap between male and female literacy is accompanied by the decreasing gap between fertility and mortality (and, hence, decreasing population growth rates).

Note that, as has been shown above (see Chapter 4), overall adult literacy turns out to be an extremely strong predictor of both male and female literacy. Overall adult literacy turns out to be a highly sensitive and effective predictor of general demographic dynamics within respective social macrosystems. The growth of overall literacy in the 0–50% range (and especially, between 5 and 30% range) would suggest rather strongly that we are dealing here with a situation in which male literacy grows much faster than female literacy, and the negative effect of overall literacy on the mortality rates[3] is extremely unlikely to be offset by the negative influence of female literacy on fertility rates. Hence, the growth of overall literacy in this range would tend to be accompanied by an increase in population growth rates.

On the other hand, the growth of overall adult literacy in the 50–100% range (and especially between 60 and 100%) predicts as strongly that we confront here the situation in which female literacy grows significantly faster than male literacy, and the negative influence of female literacy on fertility far outweighs the negative influence of overall literacy on mortality rates. Hence, the growth of the overall literacy in this range would tend to be accompanied by a quite systematic decrease in population growth rates.

That is why, though the effects of male and female literacy on demographic dynamics are rather different, it has turned out to be possible to avoid including them as separate variables into our macromodels.

We would also like to stress again that in no way are we going to claim that the literacy growth is the only factor causing the demographic transition. Important roles were also played here by such factors as, for example, the development of medical care and social security subsystems. As was discussed above (see Chapter 4), these variables together with literacy can be regarded as different parameters of one integrative variable, the human capital development index. These variables are connected with demographic dynamics in a way rather similar to the one detected above for literacy. At the beginning of the demographic transition the development of the social security subsystem correlates rather closely with the decline of mortality rates, as both are caused by essentially the same proximate factor – the GDP per capita growth. However, during the second phase, the social security development produces quite a strong independent effect on fertility rates through the elimination of one of the main incentives for the maximization of the number of children in the family.

---

[3] Of course, the proximate cause of declining mortality rates here is the growth of per capita GDP, which on the one hand leads to the elimination of such things as malnutrition, and on the other, stimulates the increase of investment in spheres other than the subsistence economy, many of which (like, first of all, the medical care subsystem) also contribute to the decrease of mortality. At first glance, education looks like just one of such "GDP-per-capita-stimulated" spheres. Note, however, that here we are dealing with a truly dynamic ("hen-and-egg") relationship, when neither variable x nor variable y could be justifiably identified as either purely dependent or purely independent. Yes, of course, the GDP-per-capita growth stimulates the development of education. But the education development also contributes in the most significant way to the GDP-per-capita growth (*e.g.*, Meliantsev 1996, 2003, 2004a, 2004b). Note that this dynamic relationship is explicitly reflected in the special extended macromodel.

The influence of the development of medical care on demographic dynamics shows even closer parallels with the one produced by literacy growth. Note first of all that the development of modern medical care is connected in the most direct way with the development of the education subsystem. On the other hand, during the first phase of the demographic transition the development of medical care acts as one of the most important factors in decreasing mortality. In the meantime, when the need to decrease fertility rates reaches critical levels, it is the medical care subsystem that develops more and more effective family planning technologies. It is remarkable that this need arises as a result of the decrease in mortality rates, which could not reach critically low levels without the medical care subsystem being sufficiently developed. Hence, whe . the need to decrease fertility rates reaches critical levels, those in need almc st by definition find the medical care subsystem sufficiently developed to sati· fy this need quite rapidly and effectively.

Let us recollect that the pattern of literacy's impact on demographic dy 1a 1-ics has an almost identical shape: the maximum values of population grow :h rates cannot be reached without a certain level of economic dev lopme t which cannot be achieved without literacy rates reaching subst mti al lev ıL. Hence, again almost by definition the fact that the system reach :d the m ɑxi-mum level of population growth rates implies that the literacy att ai ıed sı ch a level that the negative impact of female literacy on fertili ty rates w ould inc rease to such an extent that the population growth rat es would start to d ıcline. ( )n the other hand, the level of development of both medical ∶are and ₹ ocial ₹ ₹curity subsystems displays a very strong corr₀lation with ! iteracy (se e Cha pter 4). Thus, literacy rate turns out to be a very strong predic ₀or of 'ne c evelo ₁ment of both medical care and social security su`ısystems.

Note that because, in reality as we ll as in our mod₀ l, both the d ecline of mortality at the beginning of demogr ₁phic transition (₁ ₁ausing a den ₁ographic explosion) and the decline of fertility ∶uring its second phase (causing dramatic decrease of population growth rates` were ultimately produced by ₀ ssentially the same factor (human capital grow ∴h), there is there ∴fore no need fo ∙ us to in-clude mortality and fertility ₁s sepɛrate variables ir . our model. On the other hand, literacy has turned ov₀ to be a rather sensitive ∶ ndicator of the le vel of the development of human capital, which has made it ∙ ₁ossible to avoid including its other parameters as separate variables in extende d macromodels.

Conclusion

Let us start the conclusion to the first part of our introduction to social macro-dynamics with one more brief consideration of the employment of mathematical modeling in physics.

The dynamics of every physical body is influenced by a huge number of factors. Modern physics abundantly evidences this. Even if we consider such a simple case as a falling ball, we inevitably face such forces as gravitation, friction, electromagnetic forces, forces caused by pressure, by radiation, by anisotropy of medium and so on.

All these forces do have some effect on the motion of the considered body. It is a physical fact. Consequently in order to describe this motion we should construct an equation involving all these factors. Only in this case may we "guarantee" the "right" description. Moreover, even such an equation would not be quite "right", because we have not included those factors and forces which actually exist but have not been discovered yet.

It is evident that such a puristic approach and rush for precision lead to agnosticism and nothing else. Fortunately, from the physical point of view, all the processes have their characteristic time scales and their application conditions. Even if there are a great number of significant factors we can sometimes neglect all of them except the most evident one.

There are two main cases for simplification:

1. When a force caused by a selected factor is much stronger than all the other forces.

2. When a selected factor has a characteristic time scale which is adequate to the scale of the considered process, while all the other factors have significantly different time scales

The first case seems to be clear. As for the second, it is substantiated by the Tikhonov theorem (1952). It states that if there is a system of three differential equations, and if the first variable is changing very quickly, the second changes very slowly, and the third is changing with an acceptable characteristic time scale, then we can discard the first and the second equations and pay attention only to the third one. In this case the first equation must be solved as an algebraic equation (not as a differential one), and the second variable must be handled as a parameter.

Let us consider some extremely complicated process, for example, photosynthesis. Within this process characteristic time scales (in seconds) are as follows (see, *e.g.*, Riznichenko 2002):

1. Light absorption: ~ 0.000000000000001.
2. Reaction of charge separation: ~ 0.000000000001.
3. Electron transport: ~ 0.0000000001.
4. Carbon fixation: ~ 1 – 10.
5. Transport of nutrients: ~ 100 – 1000.
6. Plant growth: ~ 10000 – 100000.

Such a spread in scales allows constructing rather simple and valid models for each process without taking all the other processes into consideration. Each time scale has its own laws and is described by equations that are limited by the corresponding conditions. If the system exceeds the limits of respective scale, its behavior will change, and the equations will also change. It is not a defect of the description – it is just a transition from one regime to another.

For example, solid bodies can be described perfectly by solid body models employing respective equations and sets of laws of motion (*e.g.*, the mechanics of rigid bodies); but increasing the temperature will cause melting, and the same body will be transformed into a liquid, which must be described by absolutely different sets of laws (*e.g.*, hydrodynamics). Finally, the same body could be transformed into a gas that obeys another set of laws (*e.g.*, Boyle's law, *etc.*)

It may look like a mystification that the same body may obey different laws and be described by different equations when temperature changes slightly (*e.g.*, from 95°C to 105°C)! But this is a fact. Moreover, from the microscopic point of view, all these laws originate from microinteraction of molecules, which remains the same for solid bodies, liquids, and gases. But from the point of view of macroprocesses, macrobehavior is different and the respective equations are also different. So there is nothing abnormal in the dynamics of a complex system could have phase transitions and sudden changes of regimes.

For every change in physics there are always limitations that modify the law of change in the neighborhood of some limit. Examples of such limitations are absolute zero of temperature and velocity of light. If temperature is high enough or, respectively, velocity is small, then classical laws work perfectly, but if temperature is close to absolute zero or velocity is close to the velocity of light, behavior may change incredibly. Such effects as superconductivity or space-time distortion may be observed.

As for demographic growth, there are a number of limitations, each of them having its characteristic scales and applicability conditions. Analyzing the system we can define some of these limitations.

Growth is limited by:

1. RESOURCE limitations:

1.1. Starvation – if there is no food (or other resources essential for vital functions) there must be not growth, but collapse;
time scale ~ 0.1 – 1 year;
conditions: RESOURCE SHORTAGE.

This is a strong limitation and it works inevitably.

1.2. Technological – technology may support a limited number of workers;
time scale ~ 10–100 years;
conditions: TECHNOLOGY IS "LOWER" THAN POPULATION.

This is a relatively rapid process, which causes demographic cycles.

2. BIOLOGICAL

2.1. Birth rate – a woman cannot bear more than once a year;
time scale ~ 1 year;
condition: BIRTH RATE IS EXTREMELY HIGH.

This is a very strong limitation with a short time scale, so it will be the only rule of growth if for any possible reasons the respective condition (birth rate is extremely high) is observed.

2.2. Pubescence – a woman cannot produce children until she is mature;
time scale ~ 15–20 years;
conditions: EARLY CHILD-BEARING.

This condition is less strong than 2.1., but in fact condition 2.1. is rarely observed. For real demographic processes limitation 2.2. is more important than 2.1. because in most pre-modern societies women started giving birth very soon after puberty.

3. SOCIAL

3.1. Infant mortality – mortality obviously decreases population growth;
time scale ~ 1–5 years;
condition: LOW HEALTH PROTECTION.

Short time scale; strong and actual limitation for pre-modern societies.

3.2. Mobility – in preagrarian nomadic societies woman cannot have many children, because this reduces mobility;
time scale: ~3 years;
condition: NOMADIC HUNTER-GATHERER WAY OF LIFE.

3.3. Education – education increases the "cost" of individuals; it requires many years of education making high procreation undesirable. High human cost allows an educated person to stand on his own economically, even in old age, without the help of offspring. These limitations reduce the birth rate;
time scale: ~25–40 years;
condition: HIGHLY DEVELOPED EDUCATION SUBSYSTEM.

All these limitations are objective. But each of them is ACTUAL (that is it must be included in equations) ONLY IF RESPECTIVE CONDITIONS ARE OBSERVED.

If for any considered historical period several limitations are actual (under their conditions) then, neglecting the others, equations for this period must involve their implementation.

According to the Tikhonov theorem, the strongest factors are the ones having the shortest time scale. HOWEVER, factors with a longer time scale may "start working" under less severe requirements, making short-time-scale factors not actual, but POTENTIAL.

Let us observe and analyze the following epochs:

I. pre-agrarian societies;
II. agrarian societies;
III. post-agrarian societies.

We shall use the following notation:

– atypical – means that the properties of the epoch make the conditions practically impossible;

– actual – means that such conditions are observed, so this limitation is actual and must be involved in implementation;

– potential – means that such conditions are not observed, but if some other limitations are removed, this limitation may become actual.

I. Pre-agrarian societies (limitation statuses):
    1.1. – ACTUAL[1]
    1.2. – ACTUAL[2]
    2.1. – potential
    2.2. – ACTUAL
    3.1. – ACTUAL
    3.2. – ACTUAL
    3.3. – atypical

II. Agrarian societies (limitation statuses):
    1.1. – ACTUAL
    1.2. – ACTUAL
    2.1. – potential
    2.2. – ACTUAL
    3.1. – ACTUAL
    3.2. – atypical
    3.3. – potential

III. Post-agrarian societies (limitation statuses):
    1.1. – atypical
    1.2. – potential/ACTUAL[3]
    2.1. – potential
    2.2. – potential
    3.1. – atypical
    3.2. – atypical
    3.3. – ACTUAL

With our macromodels we only described agrarian and post-agrarian societies (due to the lack of some necessary data for pre-agrarian societies). According to the Tikhonov theorem, to describe the DYNAMICS of the system we should take the actual factor which has the LONGEST time-scale (it will represent dynamics, while shorter scale factors will be involved as coefficients – solutions of algebraic equations).

So epoch [II] is characterized by 1.2, and [III] by 3.3. ([III] also involves 1.2, but for [III] resource limitation 1.2 is much less essential, because it con-

---

[1] Systematic (not occasional short-term) starvation is caused by imbalance of technology and population, so 1.1. may be included in 1.2.
[2] According to the Tikhonov theorem, we may neglect the oscillations of population (demographic cycles), because their time scales are at least 10 times shorter than the scale of the historical period which is taken into account.
[3] Technology produces much more than is necessary for sustenance, but the growing living standards also require more resources.

cerns growing life standards, and not vitally important needs). Thus, the demographic transition is a process of transition from II:[1.2] to III:[3.3].

Limitation 3.3 at [III] makes biological limitations unessential but potential (possibly, in the future, limitation 3.3 could be reduced, for example, through the reduction of education time due to the introduction of advanced educational technologies, thereby making [2.2] actual again; possibly cloning might make [2.1] and [2.2] obsolete, so there would become apparent new limitations).

In conclusion, we want to note that hyperbolic growth is a feature which corresponds to II:[1.2]; there is no contradiction between hyperbolic growth itself and [2.1] or [2.2]. Hyperbolic agrarian growth never does reach the birthrate, which is close to conditions of [2.1]. If it was so, hyperbola will obviously convert into an exponent, when birth-rate comes close to [2.1] (just as physical velocity may never exceed the velocity of light) – and it would not be a weakness of the model, just common sense. It would be just [1.2] $\rightarrow$ [2.1, 2.2].

But actual demographic transition [1.2] $\rightarrow$ [3.3] is more drastic than this [1.2] $\rightarrow$ [2.1, 2.2]! [3.3] is reducing the birth-rate much more actively, and it may seem strange: the system WAS MUCH CLOSER TO [2.1] and [2.2] WHEN IT WAS GROWING SLOWER – during the epoch of [II]! (This is not nonsense, because slower growth was the reason of [2.1] and [3.1]).

As for the "after-doomsday dynamics", if there is no resource or spatial limitation (as well as [3.1]), then [2.1] and [2.2] will become actual. If they are also removed (through cloning, etc.), then there will appear new limitations.

But if we consider the solution of $C/(t_0 - t)$ just formally, the after-doomsday dynamics makes no sense. But this is "normal", just as temperature below absolute zero, or velocity above the velocity of light, makes no sense.

Thus, as we have seen, 99.3–99.78 per cent of all the variation in demographic, economic and cultural macrodynamics of the world over the last two millennia can be accounted for by very simple general models.

Actually, this could be regarded as a striking illustration of the fact well known in complexity studies – that chaotic dynamics at the microlevel can generate highly deterministic macrolevel behavior (*e.g.*, Chernavskij 2004).

As has already been mentioned in the Introduction, to describe the behavior of a few dozen gas molecules in a closed vessel we need very complex mathematical models, which will still be unable to predict the long-run dynamics of such a system due to an inevitable irreducible chaotic component. However, the behavior of zillions of gas molecules can be described with extremely simple sets of equations, which are capable of predicting almost perfectly the macrodynamics of all the basic parameters (and just because of chaotic behavior at the microlevel).

Our analysis suggests that a similar set of regularities is observed in the human world too. To predict the demographic behavior of a concrete family we would need extremely complex mathematical models, which would still predict a very small fraction of actual variation due simply to inevitable irreducible chaotic components. For systems including orders of magnitude higher numbers of people (cities, states, civilizations), we would need simpler mathematical models having much higher predictive capacity. Against this background it is hardly surprising to find that the simplest regularities accounting for extremely large proportions of all the macrovariation can be found precisely for the largest possible social system – the human world.

This, of course, suggests a novel approach to the formation of a general theory of social macroevolution. The approach prevalent in social evolutionism is based on the assumption that evolutionary regularities of simple systems are significantly simpler than the ones characteristic of complex systems. A rather logical outcome of this almost self-evident assumption is that one should first study the evolutionary regularities of simple systems and only after understanding them move to more complex ones.[4] We believe this misguided approach helped lead to an almost total disenchantment with the evolutionary approach in the social sciences as a whole.[5]

---

[4] A major exception here is constituted by the world-system approach (*e.g.*, Braudel 1973; Wallerstein 1974; Frank and Gills 1994; Chase-Dunn and Hall 1997; Chase-Dunn *et al.* 2003 *etc.*), but the research of world-system theorists has up to now yielded rather limited results, to a significant extent, because they avoided the use of standard scientific methods and mostly remained on the level of verbal constructions.

[5] In fact, a similar fate would have stricken physicists if a few centuries ago they had decided that there is no real thing such as gas, that gas is a mental construction, and that one should start with such a "simple" thing as a mathematical model of a few free-floating molecules in a closed vessel.

Appendix 1

World Population Growth Forecast (2005–2050)

Of course, to use our Special Extended Macromodel for prediction of future population it is better to start the simulation as close to the period of time to be predicted as possible.

Let us first check what kind of fit with observed data for the last decade of the 20th century we will have if we start the simulation with the compact macromodel in 1990.[1] The results look as follows (see Table A1.1):

Table A1.1. World Population, values predicted by the model and observed values, 1991–2003

Year	World Population, millions	
	Predicted by the Model	Observed
1991	5368.18	5368.81
1992	5451.54	5452.99
1993	5534.74	5534.93
1994	5617.72	5615.48
1995	5700.46	5696.26
1996	5782.92	5775.52
1997	5865.05	5855.07
1998	5946.83	5933.09
1999	6028.22	6009.95
2000	6109.17	6085.48
2001	6189.67	6159.70
2002	6269.67	6232.70
2003	6349.12	6305.14

$R > 0.999, p \ll 0.0001$

For the correlation between predicted and observed values of the world literacy (for 1991–1999) $R = 0.995$, $R^2 = 0.990$, $p \ll 0.0001$.

---

[1] N_0 (5284.679, in millions) and L_0 (0.696) correspond to the US Census Bureau (2005) and World Bank (2005) estimates for 1990. S_0 is taken as 1. Values of a (0.05197) and c (0.02978) are estimated on the basis of US Census Bureau (2005) and World Bank (2005) data on the growth of world population and literacy in respective year. The value of b is assumed as 0.000001.

Let us start now annual iterations in year 1999.[2] This simulation predicts the following future dynamics of the variables in question.

The model predicts the following dynamics of literacy for 2005 – 2050 (see Table A1.2 and Diagram A1.1):

Table A1.2. Future World Population Literacy, 2010–2150

Year	2010	2020	2030	2040	2050	2060	2070
Literacy	0.837	0.889	0.928	0.956	0.974	0.985	0.992
Year	2080	2090	2100	2110	2120	2130	2150
Literacy	0.996	0.998	0.999	0.9995	0.9998	0.9999	0.99998

Diagram A1.1. Predicted World Literacy Dynamics

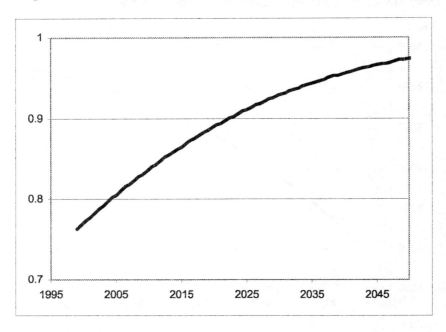

[2] N_0 (6010, in millions) and L_0 (0.7633) correspond to the US Census Bureau (2005) and World Bank (2005) estimates for 1999. S_0 is taken as 1. Values of a (0.05281) and c (0.04079) are estimated on the basis of US Census Bureau (2005) and World Bank (2005) data on the growth of world population and literacy in 1998. The value of b is assumed as 0.000001.

The model suggests that by 2050 97.4% of the world population will be literate, whereas by 2070 less than 1% of all the world population will remain illiterate.

The world population forecast generated by the model looks as follows (see Table A1.3 and Diagram A1.2):

Table A1.3. World Population, 2010–2150, millions

Year	2010	2020	2030	2040	2050	2060	2070
Population	6771.2	7324.6	7741.9	8037.3	8234.3	8358.7	8433.3
Year	2080	2090	2100	2110	2120	2130	2150
Population	8476.0	8499.4	8511.7	8517.8	8520.8	8522.2	8523.1

Diagram A1.2. World Population, 2010–2150, millions

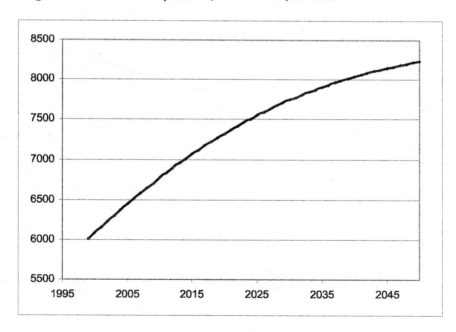

Thus, the model suggests that by 2050 the world's population will reach about 8200 million, whereas by 2100 it will more or less stabilize at *c.* 8500 million.

Appendix 2

World Population Growth Rates and Female Literacy in the 1990s: Some Observations

Our regression analysis of the World Bank (2005) and US Bureau of the Census (2005) data on the female literacy and world population growth rates has produced the following results (see Tables A2.1–2):

Table A2.1. World Population and Female Literacy, 1990–1999

Year	World Population Growth Rate (%)	World Literacy Rate, adult female (% of females, ages 15 and above)
1990	1.58	61.61
1991	1.56	62.38
1992	1.49	63.13
1993	1.44	63.90
1994	1.43	64.66
1995	1.38	65.44
1996	1.37	66.56
1997	1.32	67.71
1998	1.29	68.60
1999	1.25	69.50

Table A2.2. Correlation between World Population Growth Rate and Female Literacy, 1990–1999 (regression analysis)

Model	Unstandardized Coefficients		Standardized Coefficients	t	Sig.
	B	Std. Error	Beta		
(Constant)	4.054	0.162		25.003	0.00000001
4 Literacy rate, adult female (% of females, ages 15 and above)	-0.04044	0.002	-0.985	-160.312	0.0000002
Dependent Variable: **World Population Annual Growth Rate** (%)					

$R = 0.971$, $R^2 = 0.967$

As we see, we do observe an extremely strong and significant correlation in the predicted direction. Indeed, this regression analysis suggests that 96.7% of all the world macrodemographic variation in 1990–1999 is predicted by the following equation:

$$r = 4.05 - 0.04044F, \qquad (A2.1)$$

where F is the world female literacy (%), and r is the annual population growth rate (%).

Note that this model predicts that when the world population's literacy becomes 100% (which by definition implies 100% female literacy), the world population's growth rate will be 0.01% ($4.054 - 0.04044 \times 100$), which is extremely close to the one of the main assumptions of our compact macromodel.

On the other hand, our regression analysis of data on the female literacy and world population size for the same period has produced the following results (see Table A2.3):

Table A2.3. Correlation between World Population Size and Female Literacy, 1990–1999 (regression analysis)

Model	Unstandardized Coefficients		Standard-ized Coeffi-cients	t	Sig.
	B	Std. Error	Beta		
(Constant)	3.235	1.901		1.701	0.127
World Population (billions)	10.988	0.336	0.996	320.693	0.000000001

Dependent Variable: **Literacy rate, adult female** (% of females, ages 15 and above)

$R = 0.996, R^2 = 0.993$

This suggests the following relationship between world population and female literacy in the 1990s, a relationship quite congruent with the predictions of the compact macromodel for the same phase:

$$F = 3.2 + 11N, \tag{A2.2}$$

where N is the world population in billions, and F is the world female literacy (%).

Note that by substituting F in equation (A2.1) with the expression above (A2.2) we arrive at the following results:

$r = 4.054 - 0.04044F = 4.054 - 0.04044(3.235 + 11N) =$
$4.054 - 0.04044 \times 3.235 - 0.04044 \times 11N = 4.054 - 0.1308234 - 0.44484N =$
$3.92 - 0.44N$.

Thus, we arrive at the equation $r = 3.92 - 0.44N$, which is virtually identical with the one ($r = 3.9 - 0.44N$) produced above by the straightforward regression analysis of world population size and world population growth rates for 1990–2003 (1.1). Hence, for the 1990s the dynamic relationship between female literacy, world population size, and world population growth rate appears to produce exactly that very "inverse hyperbolic" world population growth pattern which we identified for this period at the beginning of this book.

Appendix 3

Hyperbolic Growth of the World Population and Kapitza's model

The most fundamental research in the field of global demography that describes global demographic processes as a response of endogenous population kinetics belongs to Kapitza (1992, 1999). That is, while von Foerster *et al.* (1960) pleaded for human beings to take matter into their own hands and reduce fertility, Kapitza argued for population transitions that would stem from internal population dynamics.

Kapitza's model differs from demographic models based on biological assumptions and maintaining that population growth is proportional to the population itself, which implies that mortality and fertility do not change significantly in time:

$$\frac{dN}{dt} = aN , \qquad (A3.1)$$

where *a* is a constant. Instead Kapitza follows von Foerster *et al.* (1960) to suggest using the quadratic relationship to describe the population growth rate:

$$\frac{dN}{dt} = \frac{N^2}{C} , \qquad (2.4)$$

where *C* is a constant.

Equations of type (2.4) have been studied rather thoroughly (Kurdjumov 1999) and their solutions are known as "blow-up regimes". A characteristic feature of such equations is that at a given finite moment of time t_0 their solutions go to the infinity.

As regards equation (2.4) itself, the empirically found formula (2.1)

$$N = \frac{C}{t_0 - t} \qquad (2.1)$$

(where t_0 depends on initial conditions) turns out to be just its solution.
  Indeed, take equation (2.4)

$$\frac{dN}{dt} = \frac{N^2}{C},$$

(2.4)

where C is a constant.

  Separate the variables (that is, move everything containing N to one side of the equation, everything containing t to the other) to get:

$$\frac{dN}{N^2} = \frac{dt}{C}$$

Through integration get:

$$\int \frac{dN}{N^2} = \int \frac{dt}{C} + const$$

As is known,

$$\int \frac{dx}{x^n} = -(n-1)\frac{1}{x^{n-1}} \text{ if } n \neq 1$$

(in fact this is a particular case for the following rule

$$\int x^n dx = (n+1)x^{n+1} \text{ for negative } n \text{ not equal to } -1,$$

which is inverse to the following differentiation rule $\left(x^n\right)' = nx^{n-1}$).

Thus,

$$-\frac{1}{N} = \frac{t}{C} + const,$$

hence,

$$N = \cfrac{C}{-t - \cfrac{const}{C}}.$$

The integration constant depends on initial conditions.
For the sake of convenience it can be expressed in the following way:

$$const = -Ct_0,$$

where t_0 is the same constant, but multiplied by $-C$.
Then the equation for N will be as follows:

$$N = \frac{C}{t_0 - t}, \tag{2.1}$$

where t_0 is a constant dependent on the initial conditions.

Thus, equation (2.4) describes satisfactorily the empirically found relationship (2.1), and can be used as a model of the respective demographic process.

However, though the interpretation of exponential equation (A3.1) is rather transparent and stems from the averaging-out of biological processes, the hyperbolic growth described by equation (2.4) needs explanation and justification.

Kapitza considers as the cause of the quadratic relationship between the world population size and the world population growth rate the fact that humankind constituted a single system within which one could observe paired interactions involving information exchange, whereas the growth rates of separate parts depend significantly on the overall size of the system. According to Kapitza, these are just the information interactions that constitute the main mechanism distinguishing humans from those animals among whom population growth is characterized by regularities expressed by equation (A3.1).

This way Kapitza accounts for the hyperbolic growth of world population up to 1962. As regards the solution of the second puzzle (a dramatic slowdown of the world population growth rates in the post-1963 era), Kapitza modifies his model in the following way.

As according to equation (2.4) the world population growth rate depends entirely on the population size and does not depend on any external conditions and resource limitations, the logic suggests that we look for the cause of the world demographic transition within the population itself, because for millennia no resource limitations were capable, in the final analysis, of stopping the hyperbolic growth of the world population; whereas in the present-day world, demographic transition is not caused by resource limitations, as can be seen by the fact that the dramatic decline in the relative annual world population growth rates in the recent decades has taken place against the background of growing GDP per capita. Kapitza considers as an especially important parameter what he calls "the characteristic human life-span" ($\tau = 42$ years), determined by "internal extreme capability of the human system and the human to develop".

This parameter appears in various statistical estimations; in particular Kapitza notes that the demographic transition takes place within a characteristic period of time, which equals doubled τ.

If we place in the quadratic growth equation (2.4) its solution (2.1), it can be expressed as follows:

$$\frac{dN}{dt} = \frac{C}{(t_0 - t)^2} .$$

(A3.2)

To account for the demographic transition Kapitza introduces into this equation parameter τ:

$$\frac{dN}{dt} = \frac{C}{(t_0 - t)^2 + \tau^2} .$$

(A3.3)

This equation does not produce a blow-up regime (when the solution goes up reaching infinity within a finite period of time); what is more, with this modification the world population stabilizes at the level of 10–12 billion, which corresponds not badly to the estimations of the demographers.

In addition to this, equation (A3.3) makes it possible to derive an analytical formula for the calculation of world population:

$$N = \frac{C}{\tau} arcctg\left(\frac{t_1 - t}{\tau}\right),$$

(A3.4)

where t_1 is a parameter, which equals 2000 CE (which, according to Kapitza, corresponds to the middle point of the second phase of the world demographic transition).

The research conducted by Kapitza has shown in a quite convincing way that the world population growth can be described mathematically without the introduction of any additional variables, that is actually without taking any additional factors into account. This effect creates Kapitza's grounds for proclaiming a "demographic imperative", that is the recognition of the primary and self-sufficient role of demography in the history of the development of human society.

However, neither Kapitza's basic equation (2.4) nor its modification (A3.3) describing the global demographic transition explains the mechanisms of the respective regularities; and on the phenomenological level, they remain mere assertions of empirically discovered regularities. The elegance of the "demographic imperative" makes such an approach rather attractive; in the meantime, it somehow mystifies the results obtained. What is more, from the mathematical point of view demographic data are products of the realization of some process, some integral curve, and from the mathematical point of view equations

$$\frac{dN}{dt} = \frac{N^2}{C} \qquad \text{and} \qquad N = \frac{C}{t_0 - t}$$

are equivalent, as one is nothing else but a differential form of the other.

However, notwithstanding their mathematical equivalence, the difference in the form of their expression dictates a difference in their interpretation. Thus, as was noted above, if equation (2.4), that includes just one variable N, creates preconditions for the declaration of a "demographic imperative", equation (2.1) turns out to be a departure point for eschatological conclusions formulated most evidently (though, of course, quite ironically) in the title of the first article to bring the attention of the academic community to the fact of the hyperbolic growth of world population – "Doomsday: Friday, 13th November, 2026" (von Foerster, Mora, and Amiot 1960). This suggests another thesis – the evolution of humankind is connected not with the fundamental role of demography, but with a fixed point in time, which is present in equation (2.1) as t_0. In order to emphasize the role of temporal singularity the same equation can be written in an equivalent form:

$$\frac{dN}{dt} = \frac{C}{(t_0 - t)^2},$$ (A3.5)

which, analogously to the conclusion from equation (2.4) that the population growth rate is not influenced by anything except population size, leads to the conclusion that the population growth rate is not influenced by anything except the mysterious date, Friday, November 13, A.D. 2026.

Thus, detected empirical regularities and even their successful mathematical interpolation do not necessarily give us the understanding of fundamental scientific laws, but may even lead to mystification of results. It appears that absolutization of one factor (demography, or temporal singularity) may be actually regarded as an example of excessive reductionism implying underestimation of other (and not less important) factors of development. As is known, both excessive reduction and the abstention from any reduction lead to the same result – mystification and, consequently, agnosticism. There seems to be only one way out of this situation – to find the golden mean. The system should be simplified to such a degree that the number of entered factors equals the minimum necessary for the description of observed empirical regularities; on the other hand, this number should be sufficient for clear interpretation of the relationships within the model without leading to mystification.

Bibliography

Abel, W. 1974. *Massenarmut und Hungerkrisen im vorindustriellen Europa. Versuch einer Synopsis.* Hamburg: Parey.

Abel, W. 1980. *Agricultural Fluctuations in Europe from the Thirteenth to the Twentieth Centuries.* New York, NY: St. Martin's.

Aghion, P., and P. Howitt. 1992. A Model of Growth through Creative Destruction. *Econometrica* 60: 323–52.

Aghion, P., and P. Howitt. 1998. *Endogenous Growth Theory.* Cambridge, MA: MIT Press.

Artzrouni, M., and J. Komlos. 1985. Population Growth through History and the Escape from Malthusian Trap: A Homeostatic Simulation Model. *Genus* 41: 21–39.

Berezkin 2002 – Березкин, Ю. Е. 2002. Мифология аборигенов Америки: Результаты статистической обработки ареального распределения мотивов. *История и семиотика индейских культур Америки* / Ред. А. А. Бородатова и В. А. Тишков, с. 277–346. М.: Наука.

Biraben, J.-N. 1980. An Essay Concerning Mankind's Evolution. *Population* 4: 1–13.

Bongaarts, J. 2003. Completing the Fertility Transition in the Developing World: The Role of Educational Differences and Fertility Preferences. *Population Studies* 57: 321–35.

Boserup, E. 1965. *The Conditions for Agricultural Growth: The Economics of Agrarian Change under Population Pressure.* Chicago, IL: Aldine.

Braudel, F. 1973. *Capitalism and Material Life, 1400–1800.* New York, NY: Harper and Row.

Cameron, R. 1989. *A Concise Economic History of World.* New York, NY: Oxford University Press.

Central Intelligence Agency. 2005. *The World Factbook* (http://www.cia.gov/cia/publications/factbook/).

Chase-Dunn, C., A. Alvarez, D. Pasciuti, and A. Jorgenson. 2003. Time-Mapping Globalization since the Iron Age: Three Thousand Years of Urbanization, Empire Formation and Climate Change. Paper presented at the Annual Meeting of the International Studies Association, Portland, February 27, 2003.

Chase-Dunn, C., and T. Hall. 1997. *Rise and Demise: Comparing World-Systems* Boulder, CO.: Westview Press.

Chernavskij 2004 – Чернавский, Д. С. 2004. *Синергетика и информация (динамическая теория информации).* М.: УРСС.

Chesnais, J. C. 1992. *The Demographic Transition: Stages, Patterns, and Economic Implications.* Oxford: Clarendon Press.

Chu, C. Y. C., and R. D. Lee. 1994. Famine, Revolt, and the Dynastic Cycle: Population Dynamics in Historic China. *Journal of Population Economics* 7: 351–78.

Chubarov 1991 – Чубаров, В. В. 1991. Ближневосточный локомотив: темпы развития техники и технологии в древнем мире. *Архаическое общество: узловые проблемы социологии развития* / Ред. А. В. Коротаев и В. В. Чубаров, т. 1, с. 92–135. М.: Институт истории СССР АН СССР.

Cohen, J. E. 1995. Population Growth and Earth's Carrying Capacity. *Science* 269(5222): 341–6.

DeLong, J. B. 1998. Estimating World GDP, One Million B.C. – Present (http:// www.j-bradford-delong.net/ TCEH/ 1998_Draft/ World_GDP/ Estimating_World_GDP.html).

Denison, E. 1962. *The Source of Economic Growth in the US and the Alternatives Before US.* NY: Committee for Economic Development.

Diamond, J. 1999. *Guns, Germs, and Steel: The Fates of Human Societies.* New York, NY: Norton.

Dobrynin, Djatlov, and Kurganskij 1999 – Добрынин, А. И., С. А. Дятлов и С. А. Курганский. **1999.** *Человеческий капитал. Методические аспекты анализа.* СПб.: СПбГУЭФ.

Durand, J. D. 1960. The Population Statistics of China, A.D. 2–1953. *Population Studies* 13: 209–56.

Foerster, H. von, P. Mora, and L. Amiot. 1960. Doomsday: Friday, 13 November, A.D. 2026. *Science* 132: 1291–5.

Frank, A.G., and B. Gills. 1994 (Eds.). *The World System: 500 or 5000 Years?* London: Routledge.

Grossman, G., and E. Helpman. 1991. *Innovation and Growth in the Global Economy.* Cambridge, MA: MIT Press.

Habakkuk, H. J. 1953. English Population in the Eighteenth Century. *Economic History Review* 6: 117–33.

Hatt, G. 1949. *Asiatic Influences in American Folklore.* København: Ejnar Munksgaard (Det Kgl. Danske Videnskabernes Selskab. Historisk-filologiske meddelelser, 31: 6).

Haub, C. 1995. How Many People have ever Lived on Earth? *Population Today* 23(2): 4–5.

Heine-Geldern, R. von. 1964. Traces of Indian and Southeast Asiatic Hindu-Buddhist Influences in Mesoamerica. *Proceedings of the 35th Int. Congress of Americanists* 1: 47–54.

Hoerner, S. J. von. 1975. Population Explosion and Interstellar Expansion. *Journal of the British Interplanetary Society* 28: 691–712.

Hollingsworth, W. G. 1996. *Ending the Explosion: Population Policies and Ethics for a Humane Future.* Santa Ana, CA: Seven Locks Press.

Huang, P. C. C. 2002. Development or Involution in Eighteenth-Century Britain and China? *The Journal of Asian Studies* 61: 501–38.

Jaspers, K. 1953. *The Origin and Goal of History.* New Haven, CT: Yale University Press.

Johansen, A., and D. Sornette. 2001. Finite-time Singularity in the Dynamics of the World Population and Economic Indices. *Physica A* 294(3–4): 465–502.

Jones, Ch. I. 1995. R & D-Based Models of Economic Growth. *The Journal of Political Economy* 103: 759–84.

Jones, Ch. I. 2003. Population and Ideas: A Theory of Endogenous Growth. *Knowledge, Information, and Expectations in Modern Macroeconomics: In Honor of Edmund S. Phelps* / Ed. by P. Aghion, R. Frydman, J. Stiglitz, and M. Woodford, pp. 498–521. Princeton, NJ: Princeton University Press.

Jones, Ch. I. 2005. The Shape of Production Functions and the Direction of Technical Change. *The Quarterly Journal of Economics* 120: 517–49.

Kapitza 1992 – Капица, С. П. 1992. Математическая модель роста населения мира. *Математическое моделирование* 4(6): 65–79.

Kapitza 1999 – Капица, С. П. 1999. *Сколько людей жило, живет и будет жить на земле.* М.: Наука.

Kazankov 2006 – Казанков, А. А. 2006. *Сравнительная мифология и культурная диффузия.* М.: Институт Африки РАН. (В печати).

Komlos, J., and S. Nefedov. 2002. A Compact Macromodel of Pre-Industrial Population Growth. *Historical Methods* 35: 92–4.

Korotayev, A. V., and N. L. Komarova. 2004. A New Mathematical Model of Pre-Industrial Demographic Cycle. *Mathematical Modeling of Social and Economic Dynamics* / Ed. by M. G. Dmitriev and A. P. Petrov, pp. 157–63. Moscow: Russian State Social University, 2004.

Korotayev, Malkov, and Khaltourina 2005 – Коротаев, А. В., А. С. Малков и Д. А. Халтурина. 2005. *Законы истории: Математическое моделирование исторических макропроцессов (Демография. Экономика. Войны).* М.: УРСС.

Kremer, M. 1993. Population Growth and Technological Change: One Million B.C. to 1990. *The Quarterly Journal of Economics* 108: 681–716.

Kurdjumov 1999 – Курдюмов, С. П. (Ред.). 1999. *Режимы с обострением. Эволюция идеи: Законы коэволюции сложных структур.* М.: Наука.

Kuznets, S. 1960. Population Change and Aggregate Output. *Demographic and Economic Change in Developed Countries* / Ed. by G. S. Becker, pp. 324–40. Princeton, NJ: Princeton University Press.

Lee, R. D. 1986. Malthus and Boserup: A Dynamic Synthesis. *The State of Population Theory: Forward from Malthus* / Ed. by D. Coleman and R. Schofield, pp. 96–130. Oxford: Blackwell.

Lotka, A. J. 1925. *Elements of Physical Biology.* Baltimore, MD: Williams & Wilkins.

Lucas, R. 1988. On the Mechanisms of Economic Development. *Journal of Monetary Economics* 22: 3–42.

Luria 1974 – Лурия, А. Р. 1974. *Об историческом развитии познавательных процессов.* М.: Изд-во МГУ.

Luria, A. R. 1976. *Cognitive Development.* Cambridge: Harvard University Press.

Luria 1982 – Лурия, А. Р. 1982. *Этапы пройденного пути: Научная автобиография.* М.: Изд-во Моск. ун-та.

Maddison, A. 1995. *Monitoring the World Economy, 1820–1992.* Paris: OECD.

Maddison, A. 2001. *Monitoring the World Economy: A Millennial Perspective.* Paris: OECD.

Malherbe 1997 – Малерб, М. 1997. *Религии человечества.* М. – СПб.: Рудомино.

Malkov 2002 – Малков, С. Ю. 2002. Математическое моделирование исторических процессов. *Новое в синергетике. Взгляд в третье тысячелетие* / Ред. Г. Г. Малинецкий и С. П. Курдюмов, с. 291–323. М.: Наука.

Malkov 2003 – Малков, С. Ю. 2003. Математическое моделирование динамики общественных процессов. *Связь времен* / Ред. И. Л. Жеребцов, т. 2, с. 190–214. М.: МГВП КОКС.

Malkov 2004 – Малков, С. Ю. 2004. Математическое моделирование исторической динамики: подходы и модели. *Моделирование социально-политической и экономической динамики* / Ред. М. Г. Дмитриев, с. 76–188. М.: РГСУ.

Malkov and Sergeev 2002 – Малков, С. Ю., и А. В. Сергеев. 2002. Математическое моделирование социально-экономической устойчивости развивающегося общества. *Стратегическая стабильность* (4): 54–61.

Malkov and Sergeev 2004 – Малков, С. Ю., и А. В. Сергеев. 2004a. *Математическое моделирование экономико-демографических процессов в аграрном обществе.* М.: Институт прикладной математики им. М.В.Келдыша РАН.

Malkov, Selunskaja, and Sergeev 2005 – Малков, С. Ю., Н. Б. Селунская и А. В. Сергеев. 2005. Социально-экономические и демографические процессы в аграрном обществе как объект математического моделирования. *История и синергетика: Математическое моделирование социальной динамики* / Ред. С. Ю. Малков и А. В. Коротаев, с. 70–87. М.: УРСС.

Malkov et al. 2002 – Малков, С. Ю., Ю. В. Коссе, В. Н. Бакулин и А. В. Сергеев. 2002. Социально-экономическая и демографическая динамика в аграрных обществах. *Математическое моделирование* 14(9): 103–8.

Malthus, T. 1978 [1798]. *Population: The First Essay.* Ann Arbor, MI: University of Michigan Press.

McEvedy, C., and R. Jones. 1978. *Atlas of World Population History.* New York: Facts on File.

McMichael, T. 2001. *Human Frontiers, Environments, and Desease. Past Patterns, Uncertain Futures.* Cambridge, UK: Cambridge University Press.

Meliantsev 1996 – Мельянцев, В. А. 1996. *Восток и Запад во втором тысячелетии.* М.: МГУ.

Meliantsev 2003 – Мельянцев, В. А. 2003. Три века российского экономического роста. *Общественные науки и современность* (5): 84–95.

Meliantsev, V. A. 2004a. Russia's Comparative Economic Development in the Long Run. *Social Evolution & History* 3: 106–36.

Meliantsev 2004b – Мельянцев, В. А. 2004. *Генезис современного (интенсивного) экономического роста.* М.: Гуманитарий.

Nefedov 2002 – Нефедов, С. А. 2002. Опыт моделирования демографического цикла. *Информационный бюллетень ассоциации "История и компьютер"* 29: 131–42.

Nefedov, S. A. 2004. A Model of Demographic Cycles in Traditional Societies: The Case of Ancient China. *Social Evolution & History* 3(1): 69–80.

Podlazov, A. V. 2004. Theory of the Global Demographic Process. *Mathematical Modeling of Social and Economic Dynamics* / Ed. by M. G. Dmitriev and A. P. Petrov, pp. 269–72. Moscow: Russian State Social University.

Postan, M. M. 1950. Same Economic Evidence of Declining Population in the Later Middle Ages. *Economic History Review.* 2nd ser. 2: 130–67.

Postan, M. M. 1973. *Essays on Medieval Agriculture and General Problems of the Medieval Economy.* Cambridge: Cambridge University Press.

Riznichenko 2002 – Ризниченко, Г. Ю. 2002. *Лекции по математическим моделям в биологии.* Ч. 1. Ижевск: НИЦ "Регулярная и хаотическая динамика".

Scholing, E., and V. Timmermann. 1988. Why LDC Growth Rates Differ. *World Development* 16: 1271–94.

Schultz, T. 1963. *The Economic Value of Education.* NY: Columbia University Press.

Simon, J. 1977. *The Economics of Population Growth.* Princeton: Princeton University Press.

Simon, J. 1981. *The Ultimate Resource.* Princeton, NJ: Princeton University Press.

Simon, J. 2000. *The Great Breakthrough and its Cause.* Ann Arbor, MI: University of Michigan Press.

SPSS. 2005. *World95 Database.* Chicago, IL: SPSS Inc.

Thomlinson, R. 1975. *Demographic Problems: Controversy over Population Control.* 2nd ed. Encino, CA: Dickenson.

Tsirel, S. V. 2004. On the Possible Reasons for the Hyperexponential Growth of the Earth Population. *Mathematical Modeling of Social and Economic Dynamics* / Ed. by M. G. Dmitriev and A. P. Petrov, pp. 367–9. Moscow: Russian State Social University.

Turchin, P. 2003. *Historical Dynamics: Why States Rise and Fall.* Princeton, NJ: Princeton University Press.

Turchin, P., and A. Korotayev. 2006. Population Density and Warfare: A reconsideration // *Social Evolution & History* 5 (forthcoming).

U.S. Bureau of the Census. 2005. *World Population Information* (http://www.census.gov/ipc/www/world.html).

UN Population Division. 2005. United Nations. Department of Economic and Social Affairs. Population Division (http://www.un.org/ esa/population).

Usher, D. 1989. The Dynastic Cycle and the Stationary State. *The American Economic Review* 79: 1031–44.

Verhulst, P.-F. 1838. Notice sur la loi que la population suit dans son accroissement. *Correspondance mathématique et physique* 10: 113–21.

Volterra, V. 1926. Variazioni e fluttuazioni del numero d'individui in specie animali conviventi. *Mem. R. Accad. Naz. dei Lincei* 2: 31–113.

Wallerstein, I. 1974. *The Modern World-System.* Vol. 1. *Capitalist Agriculture and the Origin of the European World-Economy in the Sixteen Century.* New York: Academic Press.

Weber 1972 – Вебер, М. 1972. *Протестантская этика и дух капитализма.* М: ИНИОН АН СССР.

World Bank. 2005. *World Development Indicators.* Washington, DC: World Bank (electronic version).

Scientific Literature and Textbooks

Popkov Yu. S. (ed.) **Dynamics of Non-homogeneous Systems.** Vol. 1–7.

Resin V. I., Popkov Yu. S. **Urban development in transitional economy.**

Bardzokas D. I., Zobnin A. I. **Mathematical Modelling of Physical Processes in Composite Materials of Periodical Structures.**

Bardzokas D. I. et al. **Wave Propagation in Electromagnetoelastic Media.**

Leschenko A. P. **The fundamental structural mechanics of elastic systems.** Book 1: Strength; Book 2: Stability; Book 3: Oscillations and flutter.

Il'kaev R. I., Seleznev V. E., Aleshin V. V., Klishin G. S. **Numerical Simulation of Gas Pipeline Networks: Theory, computational implementation, and industrial applications.**

Grigor'ev V. I. et al. **Baro-electric effect and celestial magnetism.**

Vekshin N. L. **Photonics of biopolymers.**

Kogan V. I., Galitskiy V. M. **Problems in Quantum Mechanics.**

Petrashen M.I., Trifonov E.D. **Applications of Group Theory in Quantum Mechanics.**

Borissova L. B., Rabounski D. D. **Fields, Vacuum, and the Mirror Universe.**

Rabounski D. D., Borissova L. B. **Particles here and beyond the mirror Universe.**

Postnikov M. M. **Lectures in Geometry in 5 semesters. In 7 volumes.**

Tlostanova M. **The Sublime of Globalization? Sketches on Transcultural Subjectivity and Aesthetics.**

Alexándrov P. S. **Introducción a la teoría de grupos.**

Bazárov I. P. **Equivocaciones y errores en la termodinámica.**

Malinietski G. G. **Fundamentos matemáticos de la sinergetica.**

Ivanenko D. D., Sardanashvili G. P. **Gravitación.**

Zolotariévskaia D. I. **Teoría de probabilidades: problemas resueltos.**

Galtsov D. V., Grats Iu. V., Zhukovski V. Ch. **Campos clásicos: enfoque moderno.**

Krasnov M. L. y otros. **CMS: curso de matemáticas superiores. T. 1–10.**

Krasnov M. L., Kiseliov A. I., Makárenko G. I. **CMS: curso de matemáticas superiores en problemas resueltos. T. 1–6.**

Boiarchuk A. K. y otros. **"AntiDemidóvich": matemática superior. Problemas resueltos. T. 1–10.**

Zhúkov A. V. **El omnipresente número π.**

Kolokolov I. V. y otros. **Problemas resueltos de métodos matemáticos de la física.**

Boss V. **Intuición y matemática.**

We are open to any collaboration and cooperation with authors and publishers. Your suggestions, offers, and requests for books should be sent to **URSS@URSS.ru** or to the address:
Russia, 117312 Moscow, Institute for Systems Analysis
of Russian Academy of Sciences,
Prospect 60-let Octyabrya, 9, of. 203.
Tel/Fax: 7-095-1354246, 7-095-1354216.
Internet Bookstore http://URSS.ru